Country Roads
~ of ~
NEW YORK

Deborah Williams

Illustrated by
Gloria H. Clark

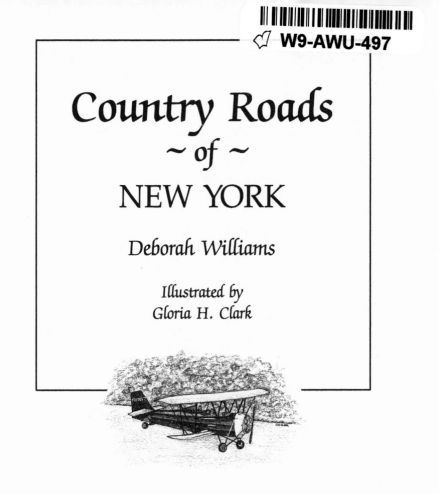

Country Roads Press
C A S T I N E • M A I N E

Country Roads of New York

Published by Country Roads Press
P.O. Box 286, Lower Main Street
Castine, Maine 04421

Text and cover design by Edith Allard.
Library of Congress Catalog Card No. 93-070217
ISBN 1-56626-018-3

Printed in the United States of America.
10 9 8 7 6 5 4 3 2

Country Roads
~ of ~
NEW YORK

*A Guide Book
from Country Roads Press*

To Marshall J. Brown and Heather Elizabeth Gang,
my favorite traveling companions

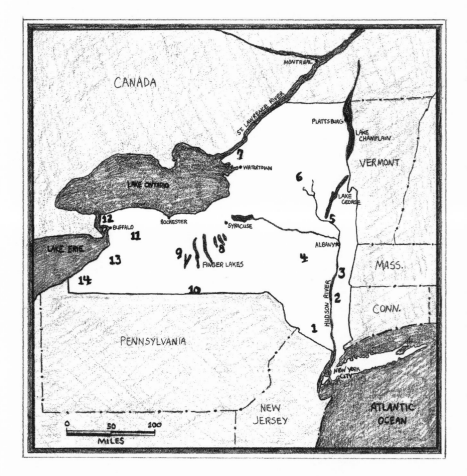

Contents

(& Key to New York Country Roads)

Introduction

New York state just may be the country's most misunderstood state. When people outside of the state think of New York, they invariably think of the Big Apple—Manhattan. To them the idea of a book titled *Country Roads of New York* is an oxymoron. Many people who live in New York City have little idea of what is beyond the limits of the city.

Contrary to the view of many Manhattanites and the rest of the world, New York state is essentially rural, abounding in country roads that travel through some of the wildest and most undeveloped regions in the entire country; roads where horse-drawn buggies are more common than gasoline-powered autos; roads than beckon travelers who care more about the route than the destination.

Some country roads in this book are long-time favorites of mine. I have traveled on them many times, in all seasons. Despite their familiarity, there were always new discoveries round the next bend, over the next hill. Others are recent discoveries, found in the course of researching this book. All have special charms and attractions that help to define the roads.

The essence of the state can best be defined in a single word—diversity. The state's agricultural bounty surprises many people. This is a top dairy state, a top producer of maple syrup, apples, pumpkins, and wine. Many of the roads in the following chapters cross through farming country.

Water has been called a region's lifeblood and New York is blessed with a bounty of lakes, rivers, waterfalls, and even seacoast. The state borders two of the Great Lakes, has mighty rivers, the Niagara, St. Lawrence, and Hudson, as well as a multitude of smaller lakes, streams, rivers, canals, and the most famous waterfall of all—Niagara Falls. Country roads crisscross and parallel these waterways.

Colonial New Yorkers bore the brunt of the Revolutionary War, and history buffs will encounter battlefields and historic sites where General George Washington battled and slept. Country roads will take you along these historic sites.

Wine lovers will discover a multitude of country roads leading to vineyards and wineries offering tastings of award-winning wines.

There are country roads for just about everyone—for those who have a day or a weekend to slow down and toss a line in a fishing stream, see the world's biggest pumpkin on the scales, pick some apples, watch ships from the far corners of the globe sail up a river, or stop to ponder where we've been and where we are going.

Pack a road map, pick a road, and go. New York is a big state and it may take a day to reach the beginning of your country road. Follow the routes described here but don't be afraid to take a detour. Country people are generally friendly and willing to direct you back or, better yet, to a new discovery up the road a spell.

To simplify road designations, I've used the following abbreviations: I=Interstate, US=U.S. Route or Highway, State=State Route or Highway.

Enjoy! I hope you can share my joy in the road not yet traveled.

1 ~

Orange County

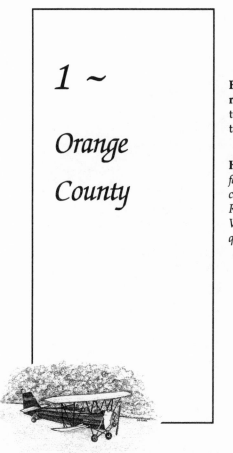

From New York and points north: Take I-87 to State 17 to US 209. From points west take State 17 to US 209.

Highlights: *Pick-your-own farms, nation's oldest winery, crafts village, West Point, Renaissance Festival, Museum Village, Washington's Headquarters.*

Orange County, which borders New Jersey and Pennsylvania to the south, the Catskill Mountains to the north, and the Hudson River to the east, abounds in country roads. The entire county is primarily farm country and small towns. Although it is within an hour-and-a-half drive of the metropolitan New York area, it is worlds away from the streets of Manhattan. Pick-your-own farms are everywhere.

A good place to begin is US 209 off State 17. Take US 209 south through the Shawangunk Mountains, and enjoy their rolling hills and small farms. Just off US 209 at Cuddebackville

1

Fishing the Delaware River

take Hoag Road to the Delaware & Hudson Canal Park. The 300-acre park includes a one-mile segment of the Delaware & Hudson Canal. The museum is located in a former blacksmith's house and features exhibits related to the canal. There are walking trails, fishing, and a self-guided tour of the canal.

US 209 continues to Port Jervis, an old river town that just about borders the three states. The Delaware River is a popular spot for fishing, canoeing, and rafting. Flo-Jean's, a historic eating establishment on the river, has been welcoming guests for more than half a century. Upstairs, customers can enjoy a view of the river and dine al fresco on the terrace in warm weather. Downstairs, there's a friendly, cozy, publike atmosphere. In Port Jervis, stop at Fort Decker on Main Street. There you will find an eighteenth-century Revolutionary War-era historic home open for tours on Saturdays from June to September and two weekends before Christmas.

Take County Road 1 east from Port Jervis through Pine Island. This is a rich, black-earth farming region that produces abundant crops of fruits and vegetables and features fields and fields of onions. During the fall migration season, geese and ducks fly overhead in formation. Mastodon bones have also been found in this area. It's easy to find a pick-your-own farm. Just watch for the signs. If you like organic produce, Dattolico Organic Farm on Mission Land Road, just two miles west of State 1, grows all its fruits and vegetables without the addition of chemicals.

At Warwick, if you are traveling during a weekend in late July through mid-September, you can continue on State 17A to Sterling Forest, home of the New York Renaissance Festival. Here you will step back into history and find knights jousting, ladies swooning, and magicians spinning their spells. There are queens and kings, Maid Marian and Robin Hood. Kids especially enjoy the mud fights, the jousting, the Punch and Judy puppet shows, and the craft demonstrations. This is a fun place to spend the day and the admission is fairly high, so plan to devote some time to this fair. You'll find plenty to keep everyone entertained for an entire day.

If you are not traveling during the Renaissance Festival season, from Warwick continue north on State 13 to Sugar Loaf, which features more than sixty-five shops, galleries, and restaurants. The tiny village, founded in 1749, is a community of craftspeople. Crafts and antique shops line Main Street. Shops are open Tuesday through Sunday. Many craft people work in their shops, and it's possible to watch works of art being created.

This is an ideal place to buy one-of-a-kind gifts and you'll find several unique toy shops—Sugar Loaf Rag Dolls and Created with Love—that have special creations for little ones. Throughout the year there are special seasonal events, including concerts, a spring and fall festival, and a Christmas caroling and candlelighting service complete with Santa. The Barnsider Taproom has been serving visitors and residents alike for generations. The Red Caboose, a bar in an authentic railroad caboose, is another good stop for refreshments.

Continue on State 13 to US 6 (which parallels State 17) into 280-year-old Goshen, the birthplace of Noah Webster of dictionary fame and President Ulysses S. Grant. In the center of town is the Trotting Horse Museum, or Hall of Fame of the Trotter, which is housed in a former stable. There you'll see more than 100 Early American oil paintings and lithographs depicting the sport of harness racing and a large collection of Currier and Ives prints. The Hall of Immortals houses dozens of small, lifelike statues that recall great trotters. Restored stalls have full-size replicas of horses and their equipment.

In late July, the Orange County Fair dominates the town of Middleton. Take US 6 to State 17M. The fair is one of the oldest county fairs in the state. It started as a small-time agricultural display in 1818 and has grown immensely, and there are now top-name entertainment and thrilling rides as well as the traditional farm animals and produce exhibits.

Back in Goshen, take State 8 to Washingtonville. Follow the signs to America's oldest winery, Brotherhood Winery. More than 150 years old, the winery offers guided tours of its cavernous underground cellars. Tours end in a wine-tasting room. All wines are also for sale by the bottle or by the case.

Lights meals are served in a small restaurant with an attractive outdoor patio.

Next take State 208 south to Monroe and Museum Village. Here is a re-creation of the daily life of preindustrial America. Open from May to December, Museum Village is a typical crossroads village of the mid-nineteenth century. Many of the buildings were rescued from other parts of Orange County and moved to the village. You'll find more than thirty-five buildings on the site, including a real blacksmith's shop where craftsmen hammer and pound the hot metal into horseshoes and door latches. There's a wagon-maker, a log cabin, a schoolhouse, and a barbershop. Horses work the fields and pull wagons. Sheep are ready for shearing. There are craftspeople at work throughout the site.

Every month Museum Village hosts special events—many with special appeal for children. Kites fly overhead and there are craft workshops and dinner on the green with costumed villagers. Kids can even buy penny candy at the general store. The Natural History Museum houses a mastodon skeleton.

From the Museum Village continue on State 17 to US 6 to Bear Mountain Bridge. Turn north on State 218 to the small village of Highland Falls and West Point, America's oldest and most distinguished military academy. Situated on the bluffs overlooking the Hudson River, West Point has been the training ground for U.S. Army officers since 1802. Here you can walk the paths of Patton, Eisenhower, MacArthur, and Schwarzkopf. Here, also, are stunning views of the Hudson River.

General George Washington recognized the strategic importance of this Hudson River location and stationed a permanent garrison of American revolutionary troops here on January 20, 1778. The goal was to thwart British efforts to control river navigation and split the colonies. A massive iron chain thrown across the sharply angled Hudson from West Point to Constitution Island prevented enemy use of the artery and figuratively bound together the struggling American states.

Links of the Great Chain are preserved and on view at Trophy Point on the academy grounds. Here, too, are cannons and relics of all American wars dating back to the Revolutionary War.

The best place to begin your visit to West Point is the visitors center, which includes displays on cadet life, a model cadet room, a theater showing movies covering a cadet's four-year stay at the academy, and the history of West Point. Just behind the visitors center is the West Point Museum with an astounding collection of sixteenth- through twentieth-century arms, uniforms, flags, military art, and West Point memorabilia. The tour begins with a look at fourteenth-century English longbows and arrows and ends with a display of the ballistic case for the "fat man" atomic bomb. There are also trophies of wars since the American Revolution. Some of the items are fascinating: the dagger worn by Reichsmarschall Goering when he surrendered to the U.S. Seventh Army, Hilter's personal handgun, and the famous letter Einstein wrote to Roosevelt urging the president to begin research on the uses of plutonium.

A poster above an artist's rendition of the faces of the four most famous American generals—Ulysses S. Grant, Robert E. Lee, Dwight D. Eisenhower, and Douglas MacArthur—sums up the West Point experience: "At West Point, much of the history we teach was made by people we taught."

It seems as if every cadet jogs rather than walks across the campus. But at 12:20 P.M. each day the entire school lines up in formation. At that time, Plebes and Yearlings (freshmen and sophomores) are quizzed by Cows and Firsties (Juniors and

and Seniors) on, among other things, the contents of the *New York Times*.

The best way to see the grounds is by foot, since driving and parking are restricted on the campus. The Plain or Parade Ground dates back to the Revolutionary War, when Baron von Steuben drilled the American forces prior to their seizure of Stony Point.

Down on the river, boat service runs on Wednesdays and Thursdays to Constitution Island, a small island off the east shore of the Hudson. During the Revolutionary War, the island had switched hands from the Americans to the British and then back to the Americans. When the war ended, the barracks were decommissioned and the island returned to civilian control. The fort structure remains intact. Part of the tour includes a visit to the home of Susan and Anna Warner, sisters and prolific writers. The house has fifteen rooms, all furnished in Victorian style.

One of the more popular exhibits at West Point is Fort Putnam, built in 1778 to protect the Hudson River and refurbished for the nation's bicentennial in 1976 using the drawings of a Revolutionary War engineer. It was threatened twice during the war, once by Benedict Arnold himself. However, the men stationed here never saw combat. Take the self-guided fort tour of weapons, casements, and redoubts recreated to look as they did more than 200 years ago.

While you are at West Point, the place to stay or dine is the Hotel Thayer, an elegant, old-fashioned hotel on the grounds of the academy. There is a comfortable feel to this hotel despite its castlelike, massive granite structure. The marble-and-wood-paneled lobby conjures up images of an earlier century. Many rooms overlook the scenic Hudson River. Our waitress at dinner entertained us with tales of the greats she has served in the dining room, including George Burns, Bob Hope, and General Norman Schwarzkopf himself—"a friendly, nice man."

If the military history of West Point has put you in a historical mood, travel north on State 218 to State 17K to Newburgh. Follow the signs that clearly point the way to Washington's Headquarters at 84 Liberty Street.

On April 1, 1782, Washington established his military headquarters in a rented fieldstone farmhouse at Newburgh, a dozen miles north of West Point, where floating barriers commanded the Hudson River. Jonathan Hasbrouck began to build this house in 1750, adding more rooms over the next twenty years to accommodate his family and to reflect his increased prosperity. Its style is typical of early Huguenot and Dutch homes in the Hudson Valley. Hasbrouck, a militia colonel who supported American independence, died in 1780. In 1782, his widow, Tryntje, and daughters moved out so that Washington could make his headquarters there.

Our guide tells us how Washington's wife, Martha, shared the house during the final months of the war. It was a close fit. In addition to the general and his wife, the house held the general's military family, which consisted of servants and two to six aides-de-camp. The aides drafted letters and channeled the flow of paperwork in and out of headquarters. The copies of letters still on the tables were tied with red tape, giving rise to the term bureaucratic "red tape," according to our guide. Mrs. Washington entertained guests in the parlor and found time for ornamental needlework, reading, and gardening.

After Washington left the headquarters for Princeton in August 1783, the Hasbroucks returned to their home. It remained in family hands until it was acquired by the state in 1849. On July 4, 1850, Washington's headquarters opened as the first public historic site in the nation. A museum was opened in 1910 to display a growing collection of artifacts. Exhibits on two floors illustrate American revolutionary and Hudson River themes. Admission is free and the headquarters is open mid-April through late October.

In the Area

All numbers are in area code 914.

Delaware & Hudson Canal Park (Cuddebackville): 754-8870

Flo-Jean Restaurant (Port Jervis): 856-6600

Fort Decker (Port Jervis): 856-2375

Dattolico Organic Farm (Pine Island): 258-4762

New York Renaissance Festival (Sterling Forest): 351-5171
(after June 1)

Barnsider Taproom (Sugar Loaf): 469-9810

Red Caboose Taproom (Sugar Loaf): 469-6031

Trotting Horse Museum (Goshen): 294-6330

Orange County Fair (Middletown): 343-3826

Brotherhood Winery (Washingtonville): 496-9101

Museum Village (Monroe): 782-8247

United States Military Academy (West Point): 938-2638

Hotel Thayer (West Point): 446-4731

Washington's Headquarters (Newburgh): 562-1195

2 ~

Along the Hudson

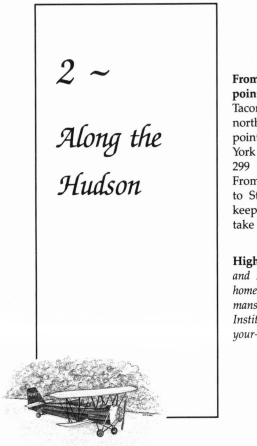

From New York City and points south: Take the Taconic State Parkway or US 9 north of Poughkeepsie. From points west take the New York Thruway to I-87 to State 299 east to Poughkeepsie. From points north take I-87 to State 299 east to Poughkeepsie and from points east take I-84 to US 9 north.

Highlights: *Eleanor Roosevelt and Franklin Delano Roosevelt homes, Vanderbilt and Mills mansions, boat tours, Culinary Institute, biplane rides, pick-your-own farms.*

This route follows the east side of the Hudson River north of Poughkeepsie through Dutchess County. If you are interested in history and grand mansions, you can visit the Eleanor Roosevelt home, Franklin Delano Roosevelt's home, and the Vanderbilt and Mills mansions. You can also take a boat tour of the Hudson River, dine at the Culinary Institute, spend the night in America's oldest inn, take a barnstorming ride in a 1929 open-cockpit biplane, enjoy magnificent views of the Hudson, shop for antiques, or pick your own red ripe strawberries and raspberries. This route would make a good leisurely weekend trip—allowing time for stops and tours.

The Hudson River dominates this drive as it dominates the area. No other river in America has played such a major role in the country's history. It has served as a major industrial waterway, gave its name to an American school of landscape painting, gave birth to the first effective steamboat, inspired writers and artists, and was the backdrop for critical battles of the Revolutionary War. The Hudson Valley has probably inspired more ghost stories that any other part of the country. It also inspired estate owners to build large manor homes—a few of which are open to the public.

Just a couple miles outside of Poughkeepsie on US 9 in Hyde Park is the Culinary Institute of America, the most famous cooking school in the United States. It's located on a seventy-five-acre, Hudson-view campus that began life as a seminary. Visitors are welcome to walk around the grounds and dine in one of the institute's award-winning restaurants. Reservations are a must for all restaurants except the informal St. Andrew's Cafe.

The next stop is Franklin Delano Roosevelt's home and the home of his wife, Eleanor, in Hyde Park. Both reveal much about the people who lived in them. FDR's wheelchair, rarely seen while FDR was alive, is now openly on display in the second-floor dressing room. Crippled by polio, the president was concerned that his image as a strong leader would suffer if people saw his wheelchair.

FDR's home gives insight into the couple's relationship. Roosevelt's mother, Sara, dominated the house. Eleanor's bedroom is small, cold, and sparsely furnished with a single bed, wicker chair, dresser, and writing table. Even while her husband was in office as president, she rarely stayed overnight here—preferring her home at nearby Val-Kill.

However, Franklin's bedroom is large and impressive, with sweeping views of the Hudson River and the distant Catskill Mountains. Some of FDR's reading material from his last days still rests on a desk in his bedroom—a March 5, 1945, *Time* magazine, a Bible, and a biography of Italian dictator Mussolini. The president usually began his day here, meeting with staff. Within easy reach are two telephones—one secretly coded with a direct line to the White House. It was used many times during the dark days of World War II.

The museum helps visitors understand this complex man. It houses the original desk and chair used by FDR in the White House. The desk is cluttered with his famous cigarette holder, donkeys and elephants given to him by his Democratic and Republican friends, miniature Scotties inspired by his own dog, and photos of his four sons in World War II military uniforms.

There are drafts of some of his most famous speeches, including his address to Congress the day after Pearl Harbor Day. The first line of his speech as he gave it reads: "a date which will live in infamy," but it originally said, "a date which will live in world history." "World history" was crossed out and replaced with the hard-hitting "infamy."

Two wings of the museum in honor of Eleanor Roosevelt were added in 1972. Some of her personal belongings are here but most are in her home—a converted factory off a dirt road— on the Hyde Park grounds. Named Val-Kill for "valley stream," the former factory building was converted into two apartments—one for Eleanor and the other for her secretary. After FDR's death she lived here full time. Begin your visit by viewing the film, *First Lady of the World.*

Although the building is plain and simple on the outside, it is warm and comfortable inside. It was here she entertained guests and her family. An otherwise perfect hostess, cooking was not her forte. Visitors will hear about the time she served her guests macaroni, potatoes, and creamed chicken with a side dish of pancakes and syrup. The screened-in porch upstairs was Eleanor's favorite place to sleep in the summer. Here she could enjoy the fresh night air and the sounds of crickets.

Just two miles north is the "cottage" of Frederick William Vanderbilt, grandson of Cornelius "Commodore" Vanderbilt. Frederick bought the neglected estate on the Hudson in 1895. "Frederick William Vanderbilt of New York," reported the *New York Times* in 1895, "who has recently joined the little colony of millionaires up the river, is getting ready to make extensive improvements on his house and grounds." Vanderbilt replaced the existing house with a fifty-four-room mansion designed by Stanford White. The *Times* described the 600-acre estate as "the finest place on the Hudson between New York and Albany."

Like most prominent Hudson River families, the Vanderbilts used their retreat only for a few weeks in the spring and fall and for occasional weekends. A staff of sixty maintained the house and grounds year-round. Vanderbilt himself loved nature and supervised the plantings on the grounds. He was proud of winning prizes for flowers, produce, and livestock at the Dutchess County Fairgrounds, and the prize money always went to the gardeners and farmhands. He planted a screen of pines and hemlocks inside the stone wall along the road that today shields the estate from modern intrusions. During our visit a deer standing tall on his hind legs was enjoying tree branches just beyond the expansive lawns. Beyond the deer and the lawns was a view of the Hudson that any millionaire or ordinary visitor could appreciate.

Vanderbilt had a passion for tapestries and they adorn the walls throughout the three-story mansion, where European royalty would feel at home. Mrs. Vanderbilt's bedroom is modeled after a French queen's bedroom of the Louis XV period. The white and gold railing around the bed follows the custom of French queens and ladies of nobility, who would hold receptions in the morning while still in bed.

Visitors come in like the upper crust and leave like the servants, our guide joked as we were led down a spiral staircase to the basement. The servants lived well at the Vanderbilt estate, and the table is set with Royal Copenhagen china.

Three miles north of Hyde Park is Staatsburg and Mills Mansion (take US 9 north to Old Post Road to the mansion). This is actually the Mills-Norrie State Park and Mills Mansion, with more than 900 acres of land along the Hudson River.

The grounds of this historic mansion are popular with the avid outdoorsperson. The grounds offer hiking trails with lovely river views and a mile-long physical fitness trail. In the winter you can fish, use groomed cross-country ski trails, and sled on the mansion's lawns and hills. There are two nine-hole golf courses, a restaurant in the clubhouse open from April to November, picnic areas, overnight camping, and a small museum.

The Greek Revival mansion was built around 1832 by Morgan Lewis, a Revolutionary War colonel and the state's third governor, and his wife, Gertrude, sister of Robert R. Livingston. It replaced another house destroyed by fire. In 1888, the home was inherited by Lewis's great-granddaughter, Ruth Livingston Mills, wife of financier and philanthropist Ogden Mills. They decided the property needed to be remodeled and enlarged, and chose the same New York architectural firm that designed the Vanderbilt mansion and many other mansions of the Gilded Age.

The result is a magnificent seventy-nine-room beaux arts mansion that the Millses used as their autumn home. If your visit is in the late afternoon, be sure to pause in the round room for a magnificent view of the sun setting over the Hudson with the Catskills in the distance.

Staatsburg is also the place to take to the river. Shearwater Cruises offers two-hour, half-day, and full-day tours of the Hudson complete with lighthouses, mansions, and beautiful riverscapes. Oceangoing freighters cruise by, carrying loads bound for Europe, Africa, or Asia. Some cruises offer gourmet lunches and dinners. The riverboats chug up and down the river from May to October.

About three miles from the Mills Mansion is Rhinebeck, a small village that traces its origins to the late 1680s, when a small group of Dutchmen purchased a tract of land along the Hudson River from a small group of Indians. Judge Henry Beekman, an Englishman, obtained a land grant from the British crown and settled here. Then German families fleeing religious persecution in their Rhine Valley came and settled. The village soon became known as "the breadbasket of New York City" as produce and other local goods were sent south on riverboats.

The Beekman Arms Hotel, the focus of activity in the center of the village, has been welcoming travelers since 1766 and claims to be America's oldest hotel. Shortly before the revolution, the old two-room inn was replaced by a larger structure and around that core the Beekman Arms has grown to its present size.

During the Revolutionary War, the entire population of the village sought refuge inside the inn's sturdy walls from an expected British attack. Although the attack never materialized, the inn has hosted Washington, as well as Lafayette and other leaders over the generations. Franklin D. Roosevelt liked to end his campaigns with a talk on the inn's porch and delivered his last campaign speech here. The 1766 Tap Room, with its huge beams and paneled walls covered with muskets, powder horns, pistols, rifles, maps, and deeds, has been offering mixed spirits for generations and is a pleasant spot for a drink. The inn serves hearty but expertly prepared American fare—the creation of noted chef and proprietor Larry Forgione. Many of the guest rooms have working fireplaces.

Rhinebeck savors history. The Dutch Reformed Church was built in 1802. Just three miles north of the center of the

A 1929 New Standard circles above the Hudson at Rhinebeck

village is the Old Rhinebeck Aerodome (take US 9 north and turn right on Stone Church Road, follow the signs to the aerodome). Aircraft here date back to the earliest days of aviation, including the 1911 Bleriot XI, the first plane to cross the English Channel and the first plane to be mass-produced, and a copy of the 1911 Curtiss "D," which daredevil Lincoln Beachey plunged into the Niagara gorge.

Time your visit for a weekend from May to October and you will be treated to an unforgettable show. On Saturdays the pioneer era of airplanes is highlighted with demonstration flights of old planes and on Sundays the battles of World War I are reenacted complete with costumes, parade, and villains galore. The shows capture the thrill and sheer fun of flying back when the Red Baron and barnstorming were popular. Before or after the shows brave souls can become barnstorm-ers themselves and ride in a 1929 open-cockpit biplane. The

16

aerodome prides itself in flying original aircraft or accurate copies powered with original engines.

Back in Rhinebeck, take time out for a drive along the tree-lined River Road. Drive south on US 9 to Mill Road. This leads into a sixteen-mile district, a contiguous landscape designated by the New York State Department of Environmental Conservation in 1980 as the first historic-scenic landscape in the state. The area abounds with outstanding examples of eighteenth- and nineteenth-century landscapes. Many of the estates are privately owned and not open to the public, but driving by gives a flavor of the estates.

Mill Road leads to County 85, which runs parallel to the river and passes through Wilderstein, the Thomas Suckley estate, which is visible through the trees. Continue along the river to Rhinecliff, a tiny hamlet whose dock offers wonderful views of the Hudson River. From Rhinecliff take River Road (State 103) north. The road passes by a number of famed river estates including Ferncliff, the former estate of William Astor. Ferncliff Forest, a 192-acre forest preserve with nature trails and ponds, is the perfect place to stretch your legs.

The next hamlet is Barrytown, named for Postmaster General Barry, who granted the community a post office in the early 1800s. It is known for the former Livingston estate Massena, which now houses the Unification Theological Seminary, operated by followers of the Reverend Sun Myung Moon. Just beyond Barrytown is Annandale-on-Hudson, which got its start as a mill town and is now home to Bard College.

River Road ends at State 9G. Continue north to Tivoli Bays, a 1,400-acre nature preserve with hiking trails. At the intersection of State 9G and State 78 (West Kerley Corners Road) turn right to US 9. If you are in the mood for fresh fruits and vegetables of the pick-your-own variety, look for the signs to Greig Farms on Pitcher Lane off US 9. This is one of the largest pick-your-own farms in the region, with almost continuous picking of everything from strawberries to pumpkins throughout the growing season. Just up the road is a magnificent herb garden where you can stop for refreshments.

Head south to the village of Red Hook, one of the earliest settled areas of the county. Antique shops abound in the village and on the roads just outside town. Stop at the Historic Village Diner, the first diner to be listed in New York's Historic Register. The Elmendorph Inn dates from the mid-1700s. The Red Hook Library is housed in the unique Octagon House.

From Red Hook complete your circle by continuing south back to Rhinebeck. On the way you'll pass the Quitman House, built in 1798. This clapboard building was constructed for Reverend Frederick H. Quitman and served as the parsonage for the nearby Stone Church until the early 1900s. It's under restoration but open by appointment for special events. The Lutheran Stone Church was built in 1786.

In the Area

All numbers are in area code 914.

Culinary Institute of America (Hyde Park): 452-9600

Franklin D. Roosevelt National Historic Site (Hyde Park): 229-8114

Eleanor Roosevelt National Historic Site (Hyde Park): 229-8114

Vanderbilt Mansion National Historic Site (Hyde Park): 229-9115

Mills Mansion State Historic Site (Staatsburg): 889-4100

Shearwater Cruises (Rhinebeck): 876-7350

The Beekman Hotel (Rhinebeck): 871-1704

Old Rhinebeck Aerodrome (Rhinebeck): 758-8610

The Historic Village Diner (Red Hook): 758-6232

Elmendorph Inn (Red Hook): 758-5887

Quitman House (Rhinebeck): 871-1798

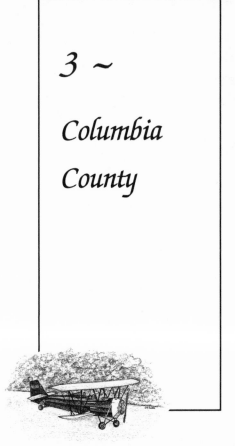

3 ~

Columbia County

From the New York City area: Take the Taconic State Parkway north to Lake Taghkanic State Park. From Albany and points west and north take I-87 to I-90 to the Taconic State Parkway. From Massachusetts and points east take I-90 to the Taconic State Parkway.

Highlights: *Lake Taghkanic, historic Hudson River mansions, antiques, Dutch homes, the Shaker Museum, firefighting museum, pick-your-own farms.*

Columbia County offers scenic views of the Hudson River, winding country roads with unexpected sights around every turn, small towns, history, and an abundance of antique shops. The county is a rural one and even the county's one city is essentially a small town.

The state park is a good place to begin your tour. Just off the parkway on State 82, it is open year-round and offers camping, fishing, swimming, hiking, cross-country skiing, and ice-skating, depending on the season. There are special events and programs throughout the year with themes like astronomy, puppets, and dinosaurs. The nature center features live displays of the fish, small animals, and reptiles that can be found in the park itself.

From the park, take State 15 south to County 8 west, to US 9 to US 6 and Clermont, the family home of the Livingstons, the patroons of a manor that at one time covered the entire southern half of Columbia County. Robert Livingston, the founder of the Livingston family in America, was born in Scotland and raised in the Netherlands. He arrived in America in 1674 when he was twenty years old. His great-grandson, also named Robert, built the present house within the walls of the original house, which was burned by the British during the American Revolution.

Livingston was appointed chancellor of New York, the state's highest judicial office. He held the post for twenty-four years and served as first U.S. secretary of foreign affairs. In 1801 he was appointed minister to France, and he negotiated with Napoleon for the Louisiana Purchase. He was fascinated with the evolving technology of the time and teamed up with Robert Fulton. Their partnership resulted in the first successful steamboat, the *North River Steamboat*, later known as the *Clermont*, in honor of Livingston. His home just may be the only home to have a steamboat named after it. On its maiden voyage up the Hudson River in 1807, the steamboat made a stop at the chancellor's dock.

The home remained in the hands of the Livingston family until 1962, when it was acquired by New York state. Now a National Historic Site, its furnishings reflect the lives of seven generations of one of New York's most influential families. There are paths and a formal garden and picnic tables and grills for your enjoyment.

Many special events are held throughout the year, including the Clermont Open Croquet Tournament, the Independence Day Celebration, Hudson River Steamboat

Days, the Pumpkin Painting Festival, and Christmas at Clermont.

About eleven miles north on State 9G is Olana, another historic home that reflects its creator's personality. Olana, derived from the Arabic word meaning "our place on high," was the home and creation of artist Frederick Church of Hudson River School fame. He bought the site after he had traveled the Americas seeking panoramic landscapes to paint. With his artistic eye, he pronounced "the views [from Olana] most beautiful and wonderful."

He had intended to model his home after a French château but a two-year sojourn in the Middle East inspired him otherwise. Your first impression of Olana as you drive up the access road that climbs 460 feet above the Hudson River is of an awe-inspiring Persian palace. It is a startling sight in the pastoral landscape. Church created Olana in the same way that he planned his art: by making pencil sketches followed by more finished color sketches. He also chose and mixed the colors for every room. Construction began in 1870, and the family moved into the second floor in 1872. The first-floor rooms required another four years to design and decorate.

Church's contemporaries regarded Olana as one of his works of art. Church created roads and planted thousands of trees. Of his landscape creations Church wrote: "I have made about one and three quarters miles of road this season, opening entirely new and beautiful views. I can make more and better landscapes in this way than by tampering with canvas and paint in the studio."

Church was clearly proud of the natural setting around his home and one of the most beautiful views can be yours by looking through the ombra, a massive window, which frames the woods, the rolling river, and the blue mountains beyond. In autumn this scene is particularly striking. Many of Church's best works hang on the walls of Olana.

Continue four miles north on State 9G to Hudson, a historic river town that claims to be the oldest chartered city in the United States. In 1783, a group of seafaring men from Massachusetts and Rhode Island were seeking a safe harbor for their vessels because of attacks by the British navy. They purchased land and began settling the area. Some of the early settlers came with houses that had been prefabricated on Nantucket in Massachusetts. Despite its distance from salt water, it soon developed into a prosperous whaling center. One of its captains, Solomon Bunker, returned with one of the largest sperm whale cargoes ever brought into the country.

As befitting a port city, Hudson had a reputation as a very sinful city. In the 1950s, the city's image was so bad that Governor Dewey sent in the state police to clean up the town. Mission accomplished, and today Hudson is undergoing a revival as an antique center for the region. The antique-shop owners have been restoring the brick Federal-period homes along Main Street. Banners proclaiming "antiques" flutter in the breeze.

This is a town that is made for walking. An hour's worth of parking will cost a nickel. Pick up a Hudson Walking Tour Guide at the Chamber of Commerce and take a walk down Warren Street, ending up at Promenade Hill, where you'll get a view of the river and Hudson-Athens Lighthouse. You'll probably get a glimpse of an oceangoing freighter traveling upriver.

Architectural historians have said that Hudson is one of the richest areas of architectural history in New York state. Number 115 Warren Street is the Seth Jenkins House, built about 1795. Seth Jenkins's father was the city's first mayor. Next door is the Robert Jenkins house, built in 1811. He also served as mayor. Stop at the beautifully restored Amtrak station just over the bridge from the river.

Before leaving Hudson, take some time to visit the American Museum of Firefighting. Turn right onto State Street, then left onto Carroll Street, which leads into Harry Howard Avenue. Bear right after Underhill Pond and the museum is on the left. Your guide will be one of the residents of the Volunteer Firemen's Home, on whose grounds this museum sits. Admission is free and the museum is filled with an amazing collection of firefighting equipment and paraphernalia.

When you first step inside you will see the museum's oldest piece of equipment: the Newsham engine, which was built in London in 1725, before George Washington was even born. This is reportedly the oldest piece of firefighting machinery anywhere in the United States. This contraption of wooden wheels and leather pipes arrived in New York in 1731 and served the people of Manhattan for 154 years.

The ornate pieces of early equipment could be considered works of art. They include a beautifully carved, piano-style fire engine built in 1851 and four panels, each adorned with a hand-painted portrait. The portraits are of New York Chief Engineer Alfred Carson and Henry Clay, George Washington, and Thomas Jefferson. A double-deck machine built in 1846 in Philadelphia resembles a circus calliope. The sides of the panel box serve as canvases: George Washington crossing the Delaware; the rescue of Captain John Smith by Pocahontas; and a female allegorical figure, the Genius of Freedom.

Pick-your-own farms are commonplace on Columbia County's roads. Take State 66 out of Hudson and turn north on State 9H. Stop at Loveapple Farm in Ghent, six miles northeast of Hudson. It's open June through December. You can pick apples, cherries, nectarines, peaches, pears, and plums in season.

Now that you are armed with baskets brimming with fruit, continue on State 9H to Lindenwald, the home of President Martin Van Buren. He was the nation's eighth president, and was born in the tiny village of Kinderhook, which means "children's corner." Henry Hudson named the village after he saw Indian children playing along the bank as he sailed up the Hudson.

Van Buren has the distinction of being the first president born under the U.S. flag. After his defeat for a second term, he gave up public life and returned to his hometown. The 1850 census listed his occupation as farmer.

The house had been built by a wealthy judge and Van Buren enjoyed making improvements in the house and grounds. He was most proud of his indoor plumbing. There

"The pure pleasure of a rural life" at
President Martin Van Buren's Lindenwald

is even a flush toilet with a Wedgewood porcelain bowl, and a zinc-lined bathtub. By all accounts Van Buren regarded his days at Lindenwald as the happiest days of his life and wrote of drinking "the pure pleasure of a rural life" there.

To maintain his "simple, elegant lifestyle" he needed servants, and he had four Irish women who lived well for the time in wallpapered rooms. They had their own sitting room and ate off British Amoy china. The entrance hall, remodeled by Van Buren, is striking with its original wallpaper depicting a French hunting scene called "Landscape of the Hunt." The guide will turn on a spotlight briefly so you can view the rich colors.

Just a mile down State 9H is the Luykas Van Alen House. This is a restored Dutch farmhouse built in 1737 and furnished with mid-eighteenth-century Hudson Valley furniture and decorative arts. The house is the oldest restoration in the Hudson Valley. It is open only from Memorial Day to Labor Day, while Lindenwald is open from mid-April to December.

Time out for a break from touring. Stop at the Treasure Shop right in the center of Kinderhook. It's a combination restaurant and gift shop filled with tantalizing aromas. The restaurant is open for breakfast, lunch, and tea, and sandwiches are made from delicious homemade bread. The pies and muffins are also baked on the premises.

The simple pleasures of the Treasure Shop should put you in the mood for the Shaker Museum in Old Chatham. The route to Old Chatham travels through picturesque little valleys lined with old farmhouses and estates. At the traffic light in Kinderhook turn right onto Hudson Street, which will become State 21. Follow the signs for Ghent. Turn right at the T intersection and keep to the right until you reach State 66. Turn left and continue into Chatham and then to a bridge in Chatham Center. Turn right just before the bridge onto State 13. The Shaker Museum is a half mile off the road on Shaker Museum Road.

The museum displays the diversity of the Shaker genius. The vast majority of the collection was acquired by John S. Williams, Sr., between 1935 and 1965, with the help of the Shaker leadership. The goal was to provide a complete picture of Shaker life and culture from as many Shaker communities as possible. There are furniture, oval boxes, baskets, buckets, and stoves, as well as complex machinery such as the first tongue-and-groove machine invented in 1828 and the patented washing machine that won a gold medal at the Philadelphia Centennial Exposition in 1876.

At their peak, Shakers numbered about 6,000, but their principle of celibacy made their future growth unlikely. Ann Lee, spiritual founder of the Shakers, directed her believers to "do all your work as though you had a thousand years to live on earth, and as you would, if you knew you must die tomorrow." That principle is expressed in the creations on display in the museum.

The orientation gallery acquaints visitors with the history of this utopian community. The annual antiques festival, one of the area's largest, is held the first Saturday in August. The complex, on forty-eight acres of rolling countryside, includes the museum shop, cafe, picnic area, and an herb garden.

If you wish to continue your Shaker-inspired wanderings, take State 13 north to US 20 east to the Mount Lebanon Shaker Village in New Lebanon just about on the Massachusetts border in the foothills of the Berkshires. Restoration is ongoing and the village is on property now owned by the Darrow School. The village was settled in the 1780s by members of the United Society of Believers in Christ's Second Appearing, or Shakers for short (after the violent trembling that sometimes overcame them during worship).

By 1930, the sect at Mount Lebanon had dwindled to five members and the property was sold to the school. Twenty-five original Shaker buildings are here. Mount Lebanon was one of the largest Shaker societies as well as the spiritual center for the sect. Several buildings are open to visitors and others will be accessible as restoration progresses.

Tim Rieman is restoring the North Family Granary. He has adapted the building, originally used to store grain, as a workshop where he creates furniture reproductions using many of the same methods used by the Shakers. Of all the Shaker furniture prized by collectors, none is more familiar than the Shaker chair or rocker. It reflects the principles that guided the lives of the Shakers: humility, simplicity, honesty, utilitarianism, and a basic uniformity.

In the Area

All numbers are in area code 518.

Lake Taghkanic State Park (Ancram): 851-3631

Clermont State Historic Site (Germantown): 537-4240

Olana State Historic Site (Hudson): 828-0135

Hudson-Athens Lighthouse (Hudson): 828-3375
(Columbia County Tourism)

American Museum of Firefighting (Hudson): 828-7695

Loveapple Farm (Ghent): 828-5048

Martin Van Buren National Historic Site (Kinderhook):
758-9689

Luykas Van Alen House (Kinderhook): 758-9265

Treasure Shop Restaurant (Kinderhook): 758-1317

The Shaker Museum (Old Chatham): 794-9100

Mount Lebanon Shaker Village (New Lebanon): 794-9500

4 ~

Leather-
stocking
Country

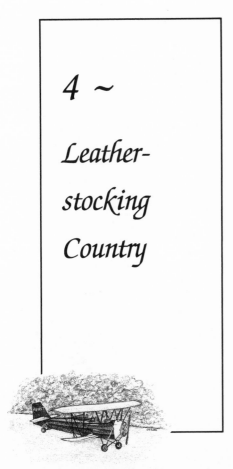

From Albany and points east and west: Take US 20 west of Albany, which parallels I-90, the New York Thruway. From New York City and points south and north take I-87 to US 20. Howe is thirty-seven miles east of Albany.

Highlights: *Howe Caverns, Iroquois Indian Museum, antique shops, Cooperstown, Baseball Hall of Fame, Farmers' Museum, opera house, lake cruises, Otsego Lake, diamond mine, Musical Museum, Cazenovia.*

Although it is possible to visit many of these attractions in a day, a weekend or longer would provide a more leisurely pace and an opportunity to enjoy the countryside and Cooperstown itself, which certainly ranks as one of America's loveliest small towns.

This is some of the most "off the beaten track" countryside in the state. It is called Leatherstocking Country—"Leatherstocking" was the nickname given to frontiersmen of the region who wrapped their legs in leather to protect them against the danger of the land as they opened the frontier, and the name was made famous throughout the world by writer James Fenimore Cooper, in his Leatherstocking Tales.

Cities are a rarity in these parts, and towns are definitely of the small-town variety. US 20 follows the old stagecoach route across the state. Traveling along US 20, take State 7 south and follow the signs to Howe Caverns. They were discovered in 1842 by Lester Howe, a local farmer who wondered why his cows stood out in the hot sun near some bushes

Cruising the River Styx at Howe Caverns

instead of under his shade trees. Upon investigation he discovered cool air blowing up out of a cave entrance behind the bushes.

After thorough exploration, he opened his cavern to the public, and it was soon heralded as a tourist attraction second only to Niagara Falls. The original descent took eight to ten hours of climbing and wading for intrepid tourists, who were provided oilskin coats and hats, rubber boots, lanterns, and a boxed lunch—all for 50 cents.

Today an elevator takes visitors 150 feet to the subterranean walkway. From there your guide will lead explorers through the caverns with stalactites and stalagmites—well-lighted by spotlights. Be sure to bring a sweater because it's cool and damp down here. It doesn't seem to be the perfect setting for a wedding, but more than 200 couples have tied the knot here, beginning with Lester Howe's daughter Elglva, who did it as an early marketing stunt. There's even a heart-shaped calcite stone set in the Bridal Altar. Legend has it that if you are single and looking, you will be married within the year if you step on the heart-shaped stone.

At one point your guide will hum into a rock and the sound will seem to come from the stalactites and stalagmites, which have grown together to form what is called the pipe organ. Then he will turn off all lights and you will be plunged into total, absolute darkness—a strange feeling, especially for those who have never experienced it before. A twenty-two-passenger boat carries you across the Lake of Venus, which is fed by the rushing water of the underground River Styx.

Just below the cave entrance is the recently opened Iroquois Indian Museum. Designed in the shape of an Iroquois longhouse, it is located in the ancient territory of the Iroquois, whose confederacy includes the Mohawk, Oneida, Tuscarora, Onondaga, Cayuga, and Seneca. Today there are approximately 80,000 Iroquois living in communities in Oklahoma, Wisconsin, Ontario, Quebec, and New York. The museum

museum hopes to serve as a unifying force for the now divided Iroquois.

If you are lucky, during your visit you can enjoy dances and musical programs performed by Iroquois. You'll find an art gallery with works of modern Indians and a gift shop with art works and crafts for sale. The children's museum was designed to allow children to experience the Iroquois way of life. They can play musical instruments, try on clothes, handle tools and furs, and make some beadwork to take home. An Onondaga storyteller is often on hand to tell traditional Iroquois tales. The museum is set in a forty-five-acre nature preserve with marked trails and a picnic area. The creators of the museum, which was ten years in the making, decided that a museum dedicated to the Iroquois belonged in a rural setting, blending in beautifully with the rolling hills and pastoral setting.

From the museum continue on State 7 to Cobleskill, particularly if you are a chocolate lover. The aroma will begin to waft through the air as you get closer to your destination— Goodbread's Chocolate Factory at 85 North Street. Here you can actually step into the factory and savor the aroma of freshly melted chocolate cooking in the kettle as confectioner Lisa Hornauer explains how candy is made. Of course, you can also buy some freshly made chocolates. The factory is in the middle of the lovely village, which boasts its own Village Historic District.

After your chocolate break take State 145 north to US 20. Sharon Springs was the site of famed mineral springs and baths. The Sharon Springs Health Spa is now on the site and offers lectures and nutritional and exercise forums.

Follow State 166 south to State 33 south to Cooperstown. While most people know Cooperstown as the birthplace of

America's favorite pastime, Cooperstown still would be celebrated as a classic without baseball. The village looks as if it was created by Disney. The village (population 2,300) boasts baskets of flowers swinging from lampposts, American flags flying from front porches filled with rocking chairs, Victorian bed and breakfasts welcoming weary travelers. These streets have changed little since Abner Doubleday pitched the first ball.

This is the town founded by William Cooper, James Fenimore Cooper's father. Cooper bought up the rights to a colonial land grant on Otsego Lake and opened the sale of land in 1786. Unlike most landowners, he did not lease land but sold it outright to encourage responsiveness to community affairs.

Stop at the Village Smithy, uphill on Pioneer Street in the village. This is Cooperstown's oldest building, built by William Cooper himself in 1786. Upstairs is the Pioneer Gallery with works of art by regional artists.

It was James Fenimore Cooper who popularized the area in his Leatherstocking Tales and it was Cooper who called Otsego Lake Glimmerglass. Discovering sites romanticized in Cooper's tales is a favorite occupation for literary buffs.

Most people do find their way to the Baseball Hall of Fame and Museum. The colonial red brick building dominates Main Street. The village is a shrine to baseball and you can feel the baseball influence everywhere. It was here in 1839 that Abner Doubleday devised the game of baseball in Farmer Phinney's field. You can see the historic ball—crude and small—with threads popped open to reveal a stuffing of rags, in the Cooperstown Room of the museum. Doubleday Field, where Abner allegedly pitched the first ball, is right in the center of town.

One room recalls World Series moments, another traces the evolution of equipment and uniforms. The overall atmosphere is like a ballpark with a turnstile at the entrance, baseball-park seats in the theater, and AstroTurf on the floor. You will see Babe Ruth's locker, Mickey Mantle's uniform, the cornerstone of Ebbets Field, box seats from Griffith Stadium, and a card collection that is the envy of every collector.

If you visit during the mid-May to mid-October season, be sure to take a cruise on Lake Otsego. Classic Boat Tours offers one-hour rides aboard the *Chief Uncas*, a sixty-foot launch built of solid mahogany for the Busch family in 1912, and on the *Narra Mittah*, a fifty-foot vessel built in 1902 for the Clark family.The captain will point out Natty Bumpo's cave, Kingfisher Tower, the source of the Susquehanna River, the Indians' Council Rock, and the historic Otesaga Resort Hotel.

The hotel fits in perfectly with Cooperstown. The name comes from an Indian word meaning "meeting place." The building is ideally located on the southern shore of the lake and just two blocks from Main Street. This is a grand old country hotel built in 1909. Every service is available, including a world-renowned golf course skirting the lake. The atmosphere is almost formal (there's a dress code for the dining room and lobby area). This is a summer hotel open only from May to October, and it is the area's largest.

There's much more to Cooperstown than baseball. Drive along State 80, which parallels the lake, to the highly acclaimed Glimmerglass Opera. Not many would expect to find a top-rated opera theater here in the rural countryside—only one of four American opera houses built especially for opera. Opened in 1987, it draws opera lovers to the shores of Lake Otsego, far from the big cities normally associated with opera. Every summer the opera mounts three productions in English. The theater side walls roll back, bringing in the beauty of the outdoors, with screens permanently in place to keep out bugs.

Almost directly across the lake is Glimmerglass State Park and Hyde Hall. It was built between 1817 and 1835 by George Clarke, owner of thousands of acres of New York farmlands, Jamaican plantations, and English coal mines. The fifty-room estate is currently undergoing restoration and is open week-ends from May to October.

Just a few miles outside of Cooperstown along State 80 is the Fenimore House Museum and the Farmers' Museum and Village Crossroads across the road. The Fenimore House is on the site of the old Cooper farm and was built in 1932 by Singer sewing machine magnate Edward Clark. The mansion houses an outstanding collection of American folk art. A smaller gallery holds works of art and memorabilia associated with Cooper. The house is open from May to December.

The Farmers' Museum and Village Crossroads, open from April to December, re-creates life in rural upstate New York between the Revolution and the Civil War. The Village Crossroads is a collection of a dozen historic buildings assembled from a 100-mile radius of Cooperstown. Sheep graze on the common and horse-drawn wagons travel through the village. Stop at the printshop to learn the latest news or visit the general store, where you can play a game of checkers and learn the latest gossip. Craftspeople give visitors a glimpse of nineteenth-century technologies at work.

From Cooperstown there are country roads in every direction that offer up interesting attractions. Just a few miles west of town on RD3 is the Waterwheel Woodworks at Dovetail Farms. This is a small country workshop where everything is made the old-fashioned way—by hand and with pride. There's a showroom in the 1810 homestead. You can design your own antique of the future. Tours are given from May to November, but the shop is open year-round.

A visit to Hogs Hollow Farm will surely delight children and pig lovers of all ages. Take State 80 west to State 51 north to Burlington Flats and watch for the signs. There are three tours a day from Memorial Day through Halloween. You'll get to hold baby pigs and help feed the sows. You can gather eggs. Country jams, honey, and lots of pig stuff fill the country store, where you can buy pork chops, bacon, sausage, fresh eggs, and even a whole or half hog. Bed-and-breakfast accommodations are also available.

During the fall, a visit to the Fly Creek Cider Mill and Orchard is a perfect way to sample the harvest of the area and see the area's oldest water-powered cider mill dating from 1856. Take State 80 west to State 26 north. It's open from late August through December.

Continue on State 26 north to State 27 to US 20 west. Fall means scarecrows in these parts, and the Butternut Barn on Allen's Lake Road in Richfield Springs hosts an annual Scarecrow Contest with every kind of scarecrow from the funny to the scary. There are also antiques and collectibles in the barn for sale.

If you want to look for diamonds—actually quartz crystals—continue on State 28 seven miles north of Herkimer to the Herkimer Diamond Mines, which are open from April 1 to November 1. You get to prospect for the quartz and keep all you find. There's also a large gem and mineral shop.

Head back to US 20 and continue west to State 12B to the tiny village of Deansboro. Here you can visit the amazing Musical Museum with a hands-on policy that encourages you to crank, pump, and play fully restored music boxes, nickelodeons, grind organs, and more. For a nickel a play, visitors can hear tunes on vintage jukeboxes from the 1900s and hurdy-gurdies from the 1700s. There are seventeen rooms full of music coming from every imaginable instrument. You'll find a shop that stocks parts, special fabrics, and information on repairing various musical antiques, and a picnic area.

Back on US 20, continue west through some of the richest stretches of antique hunting grounds in the state. You will also have a beautiful drive as the road passes over the crests of hill after hill. Picturesque valleys beckon from over every hill. An area resident claims that "driving US 20 is good for the soul."

Continue to Cazenovia, one of the region's prettiest villages. "Situation superb, fine land" were the words of John Lincklaen, agent for the Holland Land Company, when he first viewed the land at the foot of Cazenovia Lake. His elegant Federal-style 1807 mansion, with twenty acres of lawns, formal gardens, and woods, is called Lorenzo. You'll see a collection of horse-drawn vehicles and a restored carriage house. The village became the summer retreat of wealthy coastal families who discovered it after the Civil War. The lake remains the focal point of the town. The Lorenzo Historic Site, which is generally open mid-May to September, hosts a horse-drawn sleigh rally and candlelit Christmas tours in winter.

Cazenovia also boasts three very different and special country inns. The Brae Loch offers up a real taste of Scotland. The staff wear kilts and the menu features Scottish dishes and you'll find a Scottish import shop on the premises. The Brewster sits on the lake. It was built and completed in 1890 by William Brewster, a financier and partner of John D. Rockefeller, Sr., in Standard Oil. The inn sits back from the road with a broad lawn stretching down to the lake. The Lincklaen House was built in 1835 as a luxurious stopover for colonial travelers along the old stagecoach route. It has hosted such notables as President Grover Cleveland and John D. Rockefeller.

In the Area

Howe Caverns (Howe Cave): 518-296-8990

Iroquois Indian Museum (Howe Cave): 518-296-8949

Goodbread's Chocolate Factory (Cobleskill): 518-234-4842

Sharon Springs Health Spa (Sharon Springs): 518-284-2885

The Pioneer Gallery (Cooperstown): 607-547-8671

Baseball Hall of Fame (Cooperstown): 607-547-9988

Lake Otsego Boat Tours (Cooperstown): 607-547-8238

The Otesaga Hotel (Cooperstown): 607-547-9931

Glimmerglass Opera (Cooperstown): 607-547-5704

Glimmerglass State Park (Cooperstown): 607-547-8662

Hyde Hall (Glimmerglass State Park): 607-547-5098

Fenimore House (Cooperstown): 607-547-2533

Farmers' Museum (Cooperstown): 607-547-2533

Waterwheel Woodworks at Dovetail Farms (Cooperstown): 607-293-7703

Hogs Hollow Farm (Burlington Flats): 607-965-8555

Fly Creek Cider Mill and Orchard (Cooperstown): 607-547-9692

Butternut Barn (Richfield Springs): 315-858-0964

Herkimer Diamond Mines (Herkimer): 315-891-7355

Musical Museum (Deansboro): 315-841-8774

Lorenzo State Historic Site (Cazenovia): 315-655-3200

Brae Loch Inn (Cazenovia): 315-655-3431

Brewster Inn (Cazenovia): 315-655-9232

Lincklaen House (Cazenovia): 315-655-3461

5 ~

Saratoga

and

Lake

George

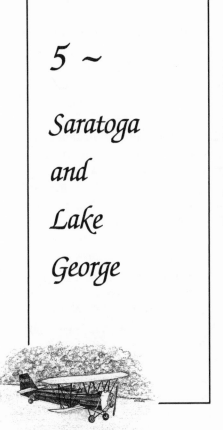

From Albany: Take I-90 to I-87 north to exit 12. From Montreal and points north take I-87 south to exit 12. From Buffalo and points west, take I-90 to I-87 north.

Highlights: *Saratoga Battlefield, Fort William Henry, Saratoga Springs, National Museum of Racing, Lake George, Fort Ticonderoga.*

This route takes in some of the state's most historic Revolutionary War sites as well as one of the state's most beautiful lakes within the unique Adirondack State Park. It would be possible to make the drive and briefly see the sights in a day, but it is best to plan on at least a weekend visit. It would be even better to plan for a longer visit, especially if you wish to take advantage of the fishing or other sports in the Lake George area.

The tour begins at the Saratoga National Historical Park and the Saratoga Battlefield—according to some historians, the most significant battle of the Revolutionary War. To get to the site take State 67 off of I-87 at exit 12. Drive east toward Malta and at Malta take State 108 east to State 9P. Follow it around the southeastern shore of Saratoga Lake. Then take State 423 east for three and a half miles to State 32 north and follow the signs to the visitors center.

Every American schoolchild learns of the surrender of General John "Gentleman Johnny" Burgoyne to the colonists at Saratoga on October 17, 1777. It was a vital and sweet victory for the colonists and certainly turned the course of history. The best way to see the whole picture is to stop at the visitors center. Here you can pick up a battlefield brochure and see the twenty-one-minute-long film *Checkmate on the Hudson*. The film has an old-fashioned tone with its regiments of toy soldiers, but it does explain the strategy and political implications of the battle.

The small museum gives a feel for the human dimensions of eighteenth-century warfare. You can see weapons, clay pipes, crude eating implements, including a wooden bowl and a little camp stove, even a toothbrush owned by the colonial soldiers. Dioramas illustrate the construction of embankments and redoubts.

There are ten stops on the well-marked auto tour of the battlefield. The complete tour is nine miles long. The road is one-way, so you can't change your mind and turn back, but you can always skip stops if you are in a hurry. There are audio tapes at most stops, each playing one to three minutes. During our visit on a fine October day, we counted twelve deer before leaving the park at dusk. As the sun set, I recalled the narrator in *Campfires of the Revolution* reading from an account of those October 1777 days: "The evening was setting in, gray and dusk; and as the nights of October are chilly in that high region, the campfires were blazing in the woods."

If you visit during the summer you will likely confront militiamen. Living history encampments are regularly scheduled at the Nielson Farm, which American generals used as their headquarters. The farmhouse still stands. During the summer there are also a variety of other living history demonstrations. Themes include: "The British and German Soldiers at Saratoga," "Songs and Ballads of the Burgoyne Campaign," "A Revolutionary Fourth of July," and "Wildflowers."

One of the more popular sites is number 7, the Breymann Redoubt. General Benedict Arnold was injured in the leg here just as Americans captured the position. The incident is immortalized by the "boot monument." This is the only monument in America that is dedicated to a piece of a hero. There's no name on the monument—reflecting Arnold's later reputation as a traitor. Had he died from his wounds here he would have gone down in history as one of America's finest generals and patriots.

"I have always thought Hudson's River the most proper part of the whole continent for opening vigorous operations," General Burgoyne wrote about his strategy for conquering the upstart colonists. "Because the course of the river, so beneficial for conveying all the bulky necessaries of an army, is precisely the route that an army ought to take for the great purposes of cutting the communications between the Southern and Northern Provinces, giving confidence to the Indians, and securing a junction with the Canadian forces."

Burgoyne's belief in the importance of the Hudson River never wavered from the moment he arrived in America in 1775. It became the centerpiece of his plan for the British northern campaign of 1777, which called for his army to move southward from Canada along the Lake Champlain-Hudson River route to Albany. Unfortunately for Burgoyne, his plan for Sir William Howe to send his army from New York City to help quell the rebellion failed to materialize.

The British general did enjoy an early victory after leaving Canada. His first major objective, Fort Ticonderoga on Lake Champlain, fell on July 6, after a four-day siege. But time and the tide of events began to run against the British, and he chose to fight the Americans at Saratoga. The battles began on September 19 and ended nearly a month later on October 17, when Burgoyne, vastly outnumbered by the Americans, surrendered. By the terms of the Convention of Saratoga, Burgoyne's depleted army with some 6,000 men marched out of camp "with the Honors of War" and stacked its weapons along the west bank of the Hudson River.

So ended one of the most decisive victories in world history. Although it would take the colonial army four more years to achieve the final victory at Yorktown, the battles here at Saratoga were very important because they occurred at a time when Americans had begun to think their cause was hopeless. The victory restored American confidence and led France to openly assist the colonists in their fight for liberty.

After your tour, you can walk 190 steps to the top of the Saratoga Monument but you will have to drive eight miles to get there first. Follow the signs for US 4 from the visitors-center parking lot and take US 4 north into Schuylerville, where US 4 becomes Broad Street. Take a left on Burgoyne Street. The monument is on the left side between Gates Street and Cemetery Avenue. The 155-foot-high monument was built from 1877 to 1883 and stands on a portion of Burgoyne's October 1777 camp. If you climb to the top on a clear day, you will be rewarded with a panoramic view of the hills and even the Hudson River in the distance.

The Schuyler House is near the monument. This estate was the country home of General Philip Schuyler both before and after the battles. Schuyler preceded Horatio Gates as the commander of American forces. The British burned the original house and its outbuildings to keep Americans from using them as cover during an attack. The present house was erected in 1777 in just three weeks, shortly after Burgoyne's surrender. There are three pieces that belonged to Schuyler: a Chippendale drop-leaf dining room table, a linen press upstairs, and a dresser in the master bedroom. Original wallpaper still hangs in the parlor, where General Schuyler entertained George Washington, Benjamin Franklin, and the Marquis de Lafayette.

The general clearly enjoyed his country life here in Saratoga. "My hobby horse has long been country life," he wrote. "I dismounted once with reluctance, and now saddle him again with a very considerable share of satisfaction, and hope to canter him on to the end of the journey of life."

From Schuylerville follow County 29 west into Saratoga Springs. If you are looking for an overnight inn within an easy drive of the attractions of Saratoga Springs, continue west on County 29 for seven miles to the small village of Rock City Falls, which boasts a number of antique shops and the Kayaderosseras River. The Mansion, a Victorian bed and breakfast, is full of antiques, elegance, and old-fashioned hospitality.

The Mansion was built in 1866 as the summer home of industrialist George West, who invented the paper bag and came to be known as the "Paper Bag King." There are four guest rooms—all with private baths upstairs and a suite downstairs with a Victorian couch from Saratoga's old Grand Union Hotel, original parquet floors, and marble fireplaces. A full gourmet breakfast is served by innkeeper Alan Churchill, who is happy to recommend sights and dining spots in town. Remember that prices for just about everything, especially accommodations, go up dramatically during August—the racing season. Count on spending about twice what you would spend during the rest of the year.

Although Saratoga Springs's glory days have gone, the town still retains much of its earlier charm. It was the place where the fashionable came to take in the spa waters, try their luck at the casino, and bet on their favorite horses. This was a favorite haunt of Diamond Jim Brady and Lillian Russell. Although the roulette wheel doesn't spin here anymore, you can still take the baths at the Saratoga Spa State Park and enjoy the horses at the track.

The history of these mineral baths goes back to the Iroquois. They closely guarded the springs until 1767, when Sir William Johnson, superintendent of Indian Affairs for the British, found his ailments and lingering war wounds almost unbearable. He was close to the Iroquois and they knew him as a honest man. Some of his Iroquois friends carried him to their spring. It isn't clear what Johnson thought of the "smelly water," as the Indians called it. However, the spa was born and others followed Johnson.

The baths are described in the spa literature: "Millions of tiny bubbles paint your body and begin their massaging action. As the bubbles burst, the natural carbon dioxide penetrates the pores of your skin, stimulating the blood flow." Your bath can be followed by a professional massage for most reasonable rates. The baths and massage are the perfect antidote for road-weary bodies. The gracious Gideon Putnam Hotel and Conference Center is also in the park.

The 2,000-acre park offers the Peerless Swimming Pool Complex with an Olympic-size pool, a diving pool, and a wading pool. You'll also find tennis courts, golf courses, ice-skating in winter, trails to walk and bike, and the Saratoga Performing Arts Center. The center is the summer home of the New York City Ballet and the Philadelphia Orchestra.

The racetrack is the oldest active thoroughbred track in the country, dating back to 1864. It hosts twenty-four days of racing each August. Breakfast at the track is a Saratoga tradition. It's served on the terrace overlooking the track early each morning while jockeys exercise their mounts. High society still thrives in Saratoga Springs, especially during the race season, when lavish balls and galas crowd the social calendar.

Just a few blocks from the track is the National Museum of Racing. During the racing season, the museum screens movies from its collection showing the thoroughbreds of yesterday and today in action. The museum is devoted to preserving articles associated with the origins and history of horse racing. On display are sculptures, paintings, trophies, saddles, and all sorts of memorabilia.

From Saratoga take US 9 north. If you are in a hurry you can take I-87, the Adirondack Northway, which has won awards for its scenic beauty. Just about twenty-two miles north of Saratoga Springs you will enter the Adirondack Park, which celebrated its centennial in 1992 and is the largest state park in the lower forty-eight states, bigger than Yosemite or Yellowstone national parks. It is also the country's most unusual and diverse park. Within its borders lie 6 million acres of mountains, lakes, streams, forests, and towns. The 2.4 million acres that are publicly owned offer recreation year-round.

The name "Adirondacks" is actually a misnomer. It came about through an expedition organized by Ebenezer Emmons, who led the state's first National History Survey in 1837. He named the mountains "the Adirondacks" after what he thought was a Huron word meaning "they of the Rock Clan." The word is actually an Iroquois term of insult meaning "bark eaters," implying that someone was such a poor hunter that he was reduced to eating tree bark. The Iroquois were forced to cede the entire property over to New York state for $1,600 after the Revolutionary War because they had backed the British.

The interior of the park remained largely unexplored and untouched until after the Civil War, when the tourist boom began. It was inspired by the first travel guide to the area, *Adventures in the Wilderness* or *Camp Life in the Adirondacks,* written by Reverend William Henry Harrison Murray. Lake George is a perfect gateway to the Adirondacks. Known as the "Queen of America's Lakes," it is 44 square miles of deep, dark blue water with 225 islands, 154 of which are state owned.

Right in the middle of the village of Lake George is Fort William Henry. It was constructed by England on a promontory overlooking the southern end of Lake George. Major General William John, the King's agent from the Mohawk Valley, ordered the fort built to block an anticipated French advance from Canada into the colonies along the Lake Champlain-Hudson River Valley route. In the summer of 1757 the Marquis de Montcalm mustered a force of 10,000 French and Indians and swept south over Lake Champlain and Lake George to confront Colonel Monro and his band of colonial defenders and British regulars.

For six days and nights, the French mercilessly pounded the log fort. Finally, Monro surrendered and the fort was completely burned and hundreds who surrendered were slaughtered. The tragedy is the central theme of James Fenimore Cooper's classic *The Last of the Mohicans,* which is a tribute to the men, women, and children who died here. The fort was completely rebuilt and artifacts that were recovered from the ashes of the fort and from the lake below are on display in the fort museum. Tours of the fort include a musket firing demonstration, a grenadier bomb-toss demonstration, a cannon firing by the Fort William Henry Artillery Crew, and a musket-ball molding demonstration, with musket balls given to the children as souvenirs of their visit. The fort looks down the length of Lake George and the view alone is worth the stop.

The village of Lake George has an old-fashioned 1950s air. Horse-drawn buggies provide rides along the streets—the horses come dressed in their own diapers. The lake boasts

46

some excellent beaches, including some prime beaches that are open to the public. The famous Million Dollar Beach on Beach Road is an easy walk from the center of the village. The name was coined because of the cost of construction and the expensive nearby summer homes.

Also on Beach Road is the Lake George Steamboat Cruise Co., which is the oldest boat-excursion company in the

The Lake George steamboat sets out for Vermont

country and has been offering passenger rides on Lake George since 1817. There are four cruise boats that travel the length of Lake George on one- to four-hour excursions. The longer cruises travel up to Ticonderoga.

If you would like a taste of Lake George elegance from another era, drive north six miles along the lake to Bolton Landing. Follow the signs and drive across a small bridge to Green Island, the home of the Sagamore. Admission is charged to day visitors but if you are staying overnight the entire seventy-acre island and resort are yours. The hotel opened in 1883 and catered for many years to a select wealthy clientele, which flocked to Lake George during the summer. In 1985, after undergoing a $72 million restoration and expansion, the 350-room hotel reopened as a luxury resort. Now listed in the National Register of Historic Places, it is open year-round and boasts a spa and indoor pool, a restored golf course, conference center, tennis and racquetball courts, and a restored wooden yacht, the *Morgan*, which provides lake cruises for hotel guests.

Fishing enthusiasts should know that Lake George has long been known as one of the great fishbowls of the Northeast. It abounds in lake trout, salmon, and bass. During a short two-hour fishing expedition with Bigfoot Charters, we caught four lake trout and released them for others to enjoy catching.

If you wish to do some antique hunting take a short detour from Lake George Village on US 9 to Warrensburg, about eight miles north. It is a pleasant, small village with several antique stores for browsing or buying.

Back in Lake George Village, take State 9N along the west side of Lake George to Ticonderoga, which can also be reached by water. You will begin to see some signs and brochures in French as you travel north and closer to the Canadian border and Montreal.

It was the French who began construction of Fort Ticonderoga. Because it is perched on a promontory overlooking both Lake Champlain and an outlet of Lake George, whoever controlled the fort also controlled travel between Canada and the American colonies. The fort has been nicknamed the "Key to the Continent." Between 1755 and 1777, it was attacked six times. Three times it was successfully held and three times it fell—a record no other fort can match.

Visitors can walk in the footsteps of George Washington, Benjamin Franklin, Ethan Allen, the Marquis de Montcalm, and Benedict Arnold. The museum contains eighteenth-century uniforms and weapons as well as unusual artifacts, including a lock of Washington's hair, Ethan Allen's pocket compass, and a rum horn given to General Schuyler by Paul Revere. You can wander through the fort independently or join a guided tour. During the summer there are dress parades, cannon firings, and fife-and-drum concerts.

Just a couple minutes from the fort is the Fort Ticonderoga Ferry. A hand-lettered sign advises that this is the departure point for the ferry to Vermont. Rutland is thirty-eight miles across the lake.

If you are enjoying a clear day, visit Mount Defiance back in Ticonderoga Village. The French called it Rattlesnake Mountain and the Americans called it Sugar Loaf Hill. Both the French and the Americans believed that it couldn't be scaled. British General John Burgoyne thought otherwise and proved himself right. He successfully fortified the hill and renamed it Mount Defiance. From there he eventually forced the Americans to flee from Fort Ticonderoga. There's now a steep, narrow paved road that leads to the top, where there are a couple of cannons. The main attraction is the view, which can be particularly glorious in the fall.

In the Area

All numbers are in area code 518.

Saratoga National Historic Site (Saratoga Springs): 664-9821

The Schuyler House (Schuylerville): 584-2000

The Mansion (Rock City Falls): 885-1607

Saratoga Spa State Park (Saratoga Springs): 584-2000

Gideon Putnam Hotel (Saratoga Springs): 584-3000

Saratoga Race Course (Saratoga Springs): 584-6200

National Museum of Racing (Saratoga Springs): 584-0400

Fort William Henry (Lake George Village): 668-5471

Lake George Steamboat Co. (Lake George Village): 668-5777

The Sagamore (Bolton Landing): 644-9400

Fort Ticonderoga (Ticonderoga Village): 585-2821

6 ~

The

Adirondacks

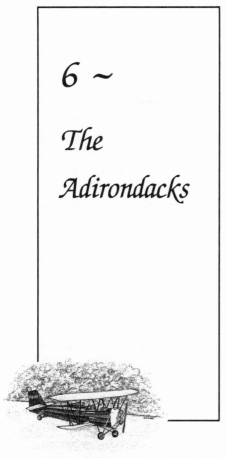

From points east or west: Take the New York Thruway to I-87 to exit 25 to State 8. From points south or north take I-87 to exit 25 to State 8.

Highlights: *Adirondack Mountains, lakes galore, remote mountaintop roads, hiking trails, Adirondack Museum, the Adirondack Lakes Center for the Arts.*

Although the route would make an easy day trip, there are so many diversions, including hiking, skiing, canoeing, fishing and just enjoying the wilderness, that most visitors will want to plan a longer visit.

This trip follows a circular route in the center of the Adirondack Park. The official boundaries of the park encompass 6 million acres, almost three times the land area of Yellowstone National Park. There are 1,000 miles of river, 30,000 miles of brooks and streams, and more than 2,500 lakes and ponds. The mountains are an estimated 1.2 billion years old and are "the survivors of the most ancient geologic formation in North America."

Take State 8 west as it skirts the south shore of Loon Lake. Just beyond Loon Lake the road crosses the Hudson River. The river actually originates to the north at Mount Marcy and the tiny, poetically named Lake Tear-of-the-Clouds.

At Wevertown take State 28 to North Creek. The small village gained fame back in September 1901 when Teddy Roosevelt, then vice-president, went climbing in the High Peaks after President McKinley was shot in Buffalo. When Roosevelt left Buffalo on September 10 for the wilds of the Adirondack Mountains and what Roosevelt called "the most remote human habitation in the Empire State," he could not have chosen a destination more likely to reassure the American people that the national crisis was over.

Of course, it wasn't over, and by September 13 the president's condition had worsened and Roosevelt was summoned from the woods. To get down to the train station at North Creek, he took the famous ride that was headlined in newspapers throughout the world. The *New York Herald* reported that leading a charge of troopers at San Juan was less hazardous that spinning through darkness along the edge of great precipices: . . . to sit miserably cooped up in a covered mountain buckboard, with none save a silent driver for witness, along frightful precipices, where a single misstep of the maddened horses meant death as surely as a Spanish bullet.

The buckboard drivers knew that Roosevelt was the new president of the United States because word had reached them that McKinley had died at 2:15 A.M., but they didn't tell Roosevelt until the harrowing ride was over.

There's a historic marker between Minerva and Newcomb that commemorates the estimated point where Roosevelt became president. The road has been renamed the Roosevelt-Marcy Memorial Highway in honor of Roosevelt. It is appropriate that the man who became president in the wilds of New York's largest wilderness preserve championed the cause of conservation throughout his life.

In mid-May every Adirondack valley has its own fern-bordered brook

Gore Mountain, just outside North Creek, with a 2,150-foot vertical rise, is the second-largest ski area in the state. Nonskiers can get in on the view from the top of Gore in the summer and fall, when the gondola operates for sightseers.

The town is also the whitewater hub of the Adirondacks and site of the annual Whitewater Derby during the first full weekend in May. The water is highest in spring after the runoff from the snow melt and appeals to the real whitewater daredevil. Hudson River Rafting Co. operates out of North Creek and offers the chance to give the river a go in a raft, inner tube, or kayak.

The drive between North Creek and Long Lake is one of the prettiest in the Adirondacks. Crowds are a rarity and there is a real feeling of getting away from it all and into the wilderness. The mountains and valleys are covered with beech, spruce, birch, and maples. The lake and mountain views are awesome and especially so in late September, when the mountains are usually at their peak of color. The foliage here can match that of any New England state. Adirondack author William Chapman described the colors of the woods and mountains: "On highland and lowland, the world is red, with all the reds from marron to madder and vermilion flaring in the sun. A hillside of maples will have 50 shades." Between Minerva and Newcomb, roads provide southern access for hikers going into the High Peaks region.

At Long Lake State 28N heads south along the east side of the lake following the Adirondack Trail. Just north of Blue Mountain Lake, State 28N becomes State 30 and continues into the village of Blue Mountain Lake. Without a doubt Blue Mountain Lake is the most beautiful village in the Adirondacks. This tiny town is a giant in the museum and cultural arena without being "touristy."

You'll find a small public beach in the village, a boat livery, a couple of stores and restaurants, and an art center.

It's smack dab in the middle of the Adirondacks and manages to remain true to itself at the same time that it offers services to the thousands of visitors who pass through each season.

Blue Mountain has less than 200 year-round residents and yet it boasts a top-notch arts center—The Adirondack Lakes Center for the Arts, which opened in 1967. Plays, concerts, and films are presented here. There are films and workshops especially for children, as well as intensive one- and two-day workshops in photography, printmaking, weaving, calligraphy, woodworking, stained glass, basketry, drawing, pottery, and painting for everyone from beginner to expert. Write or call ahead for a schedule. Crafts are a vital part of the Adirondack character and many artists, weavers, quilters, furnituremakers, and boatbuilders live in the Long Lake and Blue Mountain area. The arts center can provide a list of artists who welcome visitors.

Blue Mountain rises to a height of 3,800 feet and looks down upon the shimmering Blue Mountain Lake dotted with islands. For the best view, climb the two-and-a-half-mile-long trail to the top of Blue Mountain. On a clear day you'll have a view of 165 different peaks and 16 lakes.

Don't miss a visit to the Adirondack Museum if you are visiting between Memorial Day and mid-October. The museum is a real gem and provides insight into the entire Adirondack region and especially life in this area during the late nineteenth and early twentieth centuries. It is tucked between the lake and the mountain and offers glimpses of both.

The museum boasts 22 exhibit buildings spread out over 30 acres 250 feet above Blue Mountain Lake. It has received national acclaim as one of the finest regional museums in the country. The award-winning film *The Adirondacks: The Lives and Times of an American Wilderness* provides a good overview of the region.

A detailed set of dioramas with headsets dispenses an explanatory narrative about each scene. The Adirondack

Cottage Sanitarium was opened by Dr. Edward L. Trudeau in 1885 on nearby Saranac Lake for the study and treatment of tuberculosis. Author Robert Louis Stevenson came to Saranac Lake during the winter of 1887–88 in a futile attempt to regain his health. Although he once referred to the Adirondacks as "little Switzerland," he did not really enjoy his visit. Describing winter in the region, he wrote, "The mercury in the thermometer curls into the bulb like a hibernating bear." With the arrival of spring, Stevenson left the area for the warmer climes of Samoa.

The social heyday of the Adirondack region came after the end of the Civil War. For the first time in history, the coming of the railroad made the Adirondack region accessible to East-coast urbanites. East-coast millionaires would ship entire households of extended families to summer from June to September in rustic luxury. The museum's dioramas show these long-gone times.

"Woods and Waters: Outdoor Recreation in the Adirondacks," is the theme of one of the buildings, which could be a museum in its own right. You'll pass through simulated outdoor settings, including a simple lean-to with water rushing by, a campfire blazing, and a canoe pulled up on the shore. You will see lots of angling artifacts, a slide show that includes logging, and a hermit's cabin where you can listen to an old radio interview made with its one-time occupant, Noah John Rondeau. Another section is devoted to waterways, the principal arteries of travel through the mountains from spring thaw to winter freeze until the construction of the railroads and modern roadways.

The museum also has one of the premier collections of boats in the world. The collection includes every type of boat from sail canoes to steamboats to the famous Adirondack guide boat, used throughout the mountain country. Early in the nineteenth century, artists discovered the beauty of the

Adirondack landscape. More than 450 paintings by such artists as Thomas Cole, A. F. Tait, and Frederic Remington and 60,000 photographs are part of the museum's collection. Take a seat and watch the historic photographs pass by on a long photo belt. Adirondack rustic furniture is housed in a restored turn-of-the-century cottage.

American literature buffs will learn about the origins of Theodore Dreiser's book *An American Tragedy*, which is based on a famous murder that happened on nearby Big Moose Lake. On July 11, 1906, Chester E. Gillette clubbed his twenty-year-old mistress to death in a boat with a tennis racket and threw her overboard because she was pregnant and blocked his romance with a richer woman.

The story of the formation of laws to protect the lands and the threat to the balance of nature in the form of acid rain is told in exhibits. Acid rain has already affected the mountain lakes and forests. This is a museum that truly gives a sense of the people who have lived in and visited the Adirondacks.

It's still possible to explore the mountains, lakes, and rivers under the guidance of experienced guides. Blue Mountain Lake Guide Service offers several different types of adventures, including day rafting and week-long hunts or fishing trips.

Camping is a popular experience in the Adirondacks. However, if you wish a rustic lodge visit the Hedges on Blue Mountain Lake featuring log cabins and a central lodge with rooms and suites. Guests can use the free canoes and rowboats to explore this sparkling lake and the connecting lakes, which are perfect canoe waters.

From Blue Mountain Lake continue east along State 28 past Lake Durant, Indian Lake, Lake Adirondack, and Lake Abanakee to North Creek. From North Creek follow State 28 south. At one point the road parallels the Hudson River. The route runs into US 9 and back to I-87. From there you can travel north to Lake Placid or east to Lake Champlain or south to Lake George.

In the Area

All numbers are in area code 518.

Gore Mountain (North Creek): 251-2411

Hudson River Rafting Co. (North Creek): 251-3215

The Adirondack Lakes Center for the Arts (Blue Mountain Lake): 352-7715

The Adirondack Museum (Blue Mountain Lake): 352-7311

Blue Mountain Lake Guide Service (Blue Mountain Lake): 352-7684

The Hedges (Blue Mountain Lake): 352-7325

7 ~

The

Thousand

Islands

From Syracuse and points east and west: Exit the New York Thruway right onto I-81N to State 3. From Montreal, Ottawa, or Toronto, take State 401 east or west to the International Bridge to I-81 to State 3.

Highlights: *Lighthouses, history, battlefields, fish to be caught and to be seen in museums, romance and tragedy at Boldt Castle, boats in a museum and on the water—canoes to oceangoing freighters, wondrous views of waters around every bend.*

This tour takes in some of the most spectacular sights and vistas along the Seaway Trail, easily followed by looking for the green Seaway Trail signs. Also look for Seaway Trail War of 1812 signs—this series of forty-two clippership "War of 1812" signs marks stopping points where you will learn about the history of the war and trail. The Seaway is the longest of the national recreational trails in the United States. The entire trail is a 454-mile scenic route paralleling Lake Erie, the Niagara River, Lake Ontario, and the St. Lawrence River.

This drive begins at Sackets Harbor (take State 3 from Watertown). The village was named in honor of Augustus Sacket, a New York lawyer who in 1801 attended a land sale at the Tontine Coffee House and purchased a large tract on Lake Ontario with one of the largest natural harbors. His village was a success from the earliest days, as reported in a 1804 newspaper: "The flourishing state of Mr. Sacket's village, its advantage of water carriage and its valuable fishery renders it one of the most inviting objects to an industrious settler. . . ."

The most crucial theater of the War of 1812 was centered on the northern frontier. Here at Sackets Harbor was concentrated the great military and naval operation that successfully defended the frontier. For a time this tiny lake port was one of the most celebrated places in the nation. During the war the village developed into an extensive military complex, ringed by a fortification network manned by thousands of troops. It was the scene of heavy fighting between American and British troops. The invasion of Toronto was launched from here. The battlefield is open from May to October with guided tours. A battle reenactment is held every July, with participants sleeping in tents and wearing period costumes.

Sackets Harbor continued to prosper throughout the first half of the nineteenth century as a center of trade and commercial shipbuilding. The 156 houses and buildings from this period have been well preserved and provide a walk into history. The Augustus Sacket House, built in 1802, remains the most historic building in the village. Madison Barracks hosts historic walking tours of the limestone and brick structures, which played a part in every war from the War of 1812 to World War II.

Take State 180 out of the village past a stone bridge, where a historical marker tells all who cross that President Monroe greeted the survivors of the American Revolution at this spot. The roads are narrow and winding and tall maples form arches over them. The next stop is the tiny village of Dexter, on the Black River, with calm bays and fast-flowing waters. Originally called Fish Island because of the great fishing, it remains a fishing mecca. In the fall salmon fishing is a spectator sport. Stop at the public boat-launch site and the neighboring B & J Bait Shop to watch as arm-length salmon are brought in.

Continue west on State 12E to Chaumont, where limestone is the most prominent natural feature of the village. Chaumont quarries furnished cut stone for canal locks, lighthouses, even the Erie Canal locks.

Cape Vincent, the next village on the trail, is proud of its 300 years of French heritage. Every year on the second Saturday in July the town celebrates its rich French heritage with the Annual French Festival. Cape Vincent is named for Vincent LeRay de Chaumont, who came to America for the failing Napoleonic government, which was seeking asylum. Napoleon's chief of police built a house here in anticipation of Emperor Napoleon's escape from the island of St. Helena. He died before he could be rescued. Known as the Cup and Saucer House, it burned down some years back. Both Napoleon's sister Caroline and brother Joseph lived in Cape Vincent before returning to France.

A short detour south on Broadway (State 12) along the St. Lawrence ends at the Tibbetts Point Lighthouse. Built in 1827, it stands at the outlet of Lake Ontario and the head of the St. Lawrence River. Alas, there is no longer any need for a lighthouse keeper, since the lighthouse was fully automated in 1976. American Youth Hostel, Inc., uses the buildings on the site.

Many visitors to this area come because of the fishing, especially fishing for the huge, wily muskellunge or muskie. The record St. Lawrence muskie was caught in 1957 and weighed in at sixty-nine pounds. Evidence of the area's obsession with fish can be seen at the Cape Vincent Fisheries Station and Aquarium. Admission is free and it's open from May to October. There you will see tanks of the live fish that are found in the river and lake.

The next stop is the picturesque, old-fashioned town of Clayton, which also boasts its own Muskie Museum. If you have a sweet tooth, stop at Thousand Islands Apiaries, halfway between Cape Vincent and Clayton on State 12E. This small store has a demonstration hive where you can watch bees at work. Much of the honey sold here is produced by area beekeepers. You can buy liquid honey, honeycomb, and honey cream.

Clayton, every bit a river town, is surrounded on three sides by the mighty St. Lawrence. The dock-lined waterfront is the center for dock fishing in the warm weather and ice fishing in winter.

The Antique Boat Museum is a history and boat lover's dream. In a series of buildings on the three-acre site, the museum houses the finest collection of historic freshwater boats and engines in North America and is noted for its St. Lawrence skiff and classic powerboat collections, including the world's largest runabout, the *Pardon Me*. Boats are rebuilt and refurbished here and visitors can watch craftsmen at work. Every year on the first weekend in August, the nation's oldest Antique Boat Show brings together a magnificent collection of classic freshwater boats.

This town seems especially fond of children. The boat museum has a special area for children filled with books, puzzles, games, and a trunk full of old clothes to try on and model. Just up the street is a very large children's playground, which is a wonderful jumble of turrets and wood planks to climb and crawl over.

Clayton is also a mecca for anyone interested in traditional Early American decorative arts, including weaving, spinning, dyeing, pottery, quilting, lace and embroidery, and sculpture. Art and craft classes are offered to the public during July and August at the Thousand Islands Craft School/ Textile Museum, which is housed in one of the oldest buildings in town. Classes and workshops last from one evening to two weeks. The museum is open from April through December.

Take State 12N to Alexandria Bay, which bills itself as the "Gateway to the Thousand Islands." The Indians who inhabited the area before the European settlers arrived called the area *Man-I-To-Anna* or the "Garden Place of the Great Spirit." An Iroquois legend holds that when God summoned Eden to heaven and the garden was in its ascension, borne up by a group of white-robed angels, a thousand flowers fell from its abundance. The flowers then settled on the narrow channel of the St. Lawrence between the United States and Canada and became the Thousand Islands.

The name "Thousand Islands" is less than accurate. There are, in fact, nearly twice that number. It depends on who is doing the counting and what you consider an island. Any clump of land that could support two trees was the definition the National Geographic Society used when it counted "1,800 or so islands" a few years back.

Here the five-span, seven-mile-long Thousand Islands Bridge, linking the United States and Canada, was dedicated in 1938 by President Franklin D. Roosevelt and Canadian Prime Minister MacKenzie King. Three bridge spans are Canadian, one is American, and one is international. The International Rift span across the border is ninety feet long, and it is the shortest international vehicular bridge in the world.

Just before the bridge, look for signs to Wellesley Island State Park. The 600-acre Minna Anthony Common Nature

Center in the park has eight miles of trails, special trails for the disabled, and a Nature Center Museum. Trails are well marked. Take the two-and-a-half-mile-long Eel Bay Loop for scenic views of Eel Bay and the Narrows.

At one time, the most exclusive club in the world was the Thousand Islands Club on Wellesley Island. The initiation fee was $100,000 and the annual fee was $10,000. Because the border between Canada and the United States is a mass of islands, fugitives have long relished this region as a haven from authorities. During the late 1970s "Barry Freed" lived on Wellesley Island and became active in local environmental causes. Locals were taken aback to discover in 1980 that Barry Freed was actually the fugitive student radical Abbie Hoffman, who had jumped bail in 1974. He later surrendered to authorities in New York.

For a dramatic view of many islands, continue across the next span of the bridge to Hill Island, Ontario, and the Thousand Islands Skydeck. You will travel upwards in an express elevator that takes forty seconds to reach the glass-enclosed deck at the 320-foot level—on a clear day you will be able to see about forty miles. You may climb up to the open-air deck or even higher to the crow's nest. If this isn't high enough, take a ride in a helicopter with Thousand Islands Helicopter Tours on State 12 just before the village of Alexandria Bay.

Although summer is the most popular season for tourists, autumn is particularly special, with glorious colors reflecting in the blue waters. During the fall migration season, the region serves as a major staging area for tens of thousands of ducks and geese on their southbound journey.

To get a real taste of the Thousand Islands it's necessary to abandon the auto and take to the water. If you don't have a boat of your own, Empire Boat Tours and Uncle Sam Boat Tours provide guided tours of the river and the islands. At the beginning of this century financial barons vied with one another in building sumptuous summer estates on their own private islands. The most outstanding of all is the signature structure of the islands—Boldt Castle. Tour boats stop at the castle, which is open for tours from May through Columbus Day.

Hollywood could not have dreamed up a more romantic-tragic story than the tale of the castle and its creator. George C. Boldt came to America from Prussia at age thirteen in 1864. In time he became the most famous hotel magnate in the world—in charge of the Waldorf-Astoria in New York and the Bellevue-Stratford in Philadelphia. He and his wife, Louise, came to the Thousand Islands on vacation and he decided to buy an island and create a castle to show his love for his wife. He even had the island reshaped to resemble a heart. Hearts are integrated in design elements throughout the castle. Boldt spent more than $2 million before tragedy struck and his wife died in January 1904. Heartsick, he ordered the 300 workmen

Hearts adorn the castle
George C. Boldt built
for his beloved wife

to leave and he never returned. The unfinished structure stands in all its haunting majesty. The rooms are empty and the ill-fated castle has a certain melancholy air. It's a symbol of what might have been had death not cut short a man's dreams.

Boat captains will point out other Thousand Island oddities. You'll pass Zavicon Island, which boasts the shortest (forty-two-feet-long and five-feet-wide) international bridge in the world, connecting two islands—one in Canadian and the other in U.S. waters. There are forty-five Canadian and New York state parks in the Thousand Islands region. Several are accessible only by boat. Another attraction is Price is Right Island, which was given away in 1964 by Bill Cullen on the "Price is Right" television program. Of course, Thousand Island salad dressing originated in the islands and gained fame when George Boldt began using the dressing in his hotels.

The Cornwall Brothers Store, down on the village's waterfront, is a pictorial history of the grand days of river life. The store was originally owned by Azariah Walton, a founding father of Alexandria Bay who saw the advantage of establishing a waterfront business. The early 1800s saw the rise of the steamship era, when all waterfront towns were used as "wooding stations" to accommodate the large steamers, which burned wood rapidly.

Continue following the Seaway Trail along the river about thirty-five miles north to Ogdensburg, the oldest settlement in the area. Its 1809 custom house is the oldest active federal building in the United States. The big attraction in town is the Remington Museum at 303 Washington Street. Although artist Frederic Remington gained fame as a painter of the American West, he was born in nearby Canton. This museum houses more than 200 of his works, the largest collection in the country.

If you're interested in ships and locks, the trail continues another forty-five miles north along the river on State 37 to Massena, where the big attraction is the Eisenhower Lock. Huge cargo vessels pass on their way from across the ocean and the heartland of America. The process of getting a ship through the lock takes about forty-five minutes—raising or lowering a ship by forty feet requires the displacement of an incredible 22 million gallons of water. To be sure you'll see the lock in action, call ahead (315-769-2422) to find out what time a ship is scheduled to pass through. During the nine-month season, traffic is fairly steady.

Another fifteen miles north you'll see a bridge across the river to Ontario or the border crossing to Quebec. *Bon voyage!*

In the Area

All numbers are in area code 315.

Sackets Harbor Battlefield State Historic Site (Sackets Harbor): 646-3634

Madison Barracks (Sackets Harbor): 646-3374

B & J Bait Shop (Dexter): 639-3686

Tibbetts Point Lighthouse (Cape Vincent): 654-3450

Cape Vincent Fisheries Station and Aquarium (Cape Vincent): 654-2147

Muskie Museum (Clayton): 686-5794

Thousand Islands Apiaries (Clayton): 654-2741

Antique Boat Museum (Clayton): 686-4104

Thousand Islands Craft School/Textile Museum (Clayton): 686-4123

Wellesley Island State Park (Alexandria Bay): 482-2722

Minna Anthony Common Nature Center (Alexandria Bay): 482-2479

Thousand Islands Helicopter Tours (Alexandria Bay): 482-5722

Empire Boat Tours (Alexandria Bay): 482-9511

Uncle Sam Boat Tours (Alexandria Bay): 482-2611

Boldt Castle (Alexandria Bay): 800-8ISLAND

Cornwall Brothers Store (Alexandria Bay): 482-4586

Remington Museum (Ogdensburg): 393-2425

Eisenhower Lock (Massena): 769-2422

8 ~

The

Finger

Lakes

From points north: Take I-81 to I-690 to Liverpool. From points east and west take the New York Thruway (I-90) to I-690 to Liverpool. From points south, take I-81 to I-690 to Liverpool

Highlights: *French fort, lovely villages, polo matches, Tiffany chapel, William Seward's home.*

This tour begins in the seventeenth century at a re-creation of a French fort on the shores of Lake Onondaga, in the village of Liverpool, north of Syracuse. From there, the tour continues south to what could easily rank as the loveliest village in a region that abounds in lovely villages. You can take in an afternoon polo match, take a ride around Skaneateles Lake with the U.S. mail, visit the only complete and unaltered Tiffany chapel known to exist, and see the home of William Seward, who negotiated the purchase of Alaska. This could be an easy day trip, although for those who wish to extend their tour there are comfortable historic country inns that have been welcoming travelers for generations.

"You must have had a long journey." That's the friendly welcome you'll receive as you walk into the mission and the seventeenth century at Sainte Marie Among the Iroquois, sitting high above Onondaga Lake in Liverpool. However long your journey has been, it cannot compare to those of seventeenth-century travelers who endured hardships and dangers to reach the mission.

In 1654, Father Simon Le Moyne, a French Jesuit, traveled from Quebec to arrange a peace treaty with the Onondaga Indians, also known as the Haudenosaunee, who were part of the Iroquois Nation. The Indians showed Le Moyne a salt spring on the shore of the Gannentaha, better known today as Onondaga Lake. Two years later, about fifty Frenchmen returned to the salt spring to build a mission settlement.

A number of Iroquois did not welcome the French and they decided to force the French to leave. Forewarned by an Iroquois spy, the French arranged a successful escape. They invited the Indians to a big feast, entertained and fed them constantly to keep them awake, and then escaped once the Indians finally fell asleep in exhaustion. The plan worked and the French missionaries escaped safely, but the mission was abandoned and the French never returned to central New York.

In 1933 WPA workers reconstructed the mission. Unfortunately, the rebuilt structure was historically inaccurate in many ways. In the mid-1980s the fort was completely run-down and Onondaga County decided to rebuild and present the history of the mission and the area from both the European and Native American points of view. A visitors center was built to serve as a physical and explanatory bridge between the new and the old worlds. The result is an entertaining, educational museum and historical re-creation that succeeds in its mission.

The staff in the mission are first-person interpreters, meaning they are the characters they portray and cannot step out of character and into the twentieth century. The interpreters spend one day a week researching the character, furniture, and procedures of the seventeenth century to ensure historical accuracy.

Although it just takes a minute to walk from the visitors center to the seventeenth-century mission, the transformation is quite amazing. A dirt path leads to the mission. Outside the walls are a vegetable garden and a cornfield planted Indian-style with beans, pumpkins, and squash around the corn.

Inside the walls of the mission, a Jesuit priest describes the arduous two-month trip from Quebec as he readies the small chapel. Led by Iroquois guides, seven Jesuits, twelve soldiers, and thirty craftsmen and workers traveled in twenty canoes into the unknown wilderness. Major Zacharie Dupois, commander of the settlement, bids you *bienvenue,* or welcome, at the doorway to the cookhouse. An apprentice cook is mixing bread. A wooden table with long benches stands along one wall. The men of the mission cooked, ate, and slept in this building.

The mission overlooks Onondaga Lake Park, which extends for six miles along the eastern shore of the lake. The park has picnic sites, a marina, and harbor, as well as the original Le Moyne Salt Spring. Tram tours and bike rentals are available. Here, also, is the Salt Museum, which has exhibits and a reconstructed 1856 salt factory where salt processing is demonstrated. The museum is housed in a replica of an early salt block and focuses primarily on the salt industry during the Industrial Revolution.

From the lake, take I-690 to State 5 west to State 174. This route goes through Camillus and Marcellus, two pretty little villages west of Syracuse. Continue on State 174 to US 20, the old stagecoach route, which cuts across the state and takes the traveler into Skaneateles.

Although Finger Lakes aficionados have their favorite lakes and towns, most would agree that the village of Skaneateles on the northern tip of the fifteen-mile-long lake ranks as the loveliest of all the region's picturesque villages. William H. Seward, secretary of state under Lincoln and later Johnson, who lived in nearby Auburn, called Skaneateles Lake "the most beautiful body of water in the world" after a trip around the world.

The Sherwood Inn has been welcoming travelers for generations. It was 1807 when Isaac Sherwood, a giant of a man said to tip the scales at well over 300 pounds, built a tavern here as a way station along his stagecoach route carrying passengers and goods from Auburn seven miles west and Syracuse nineteen miles northeast. Travelers on the stagecoach route between New York City and Niagara Falls found Skaneateles, about halfway between the two points, an ideal stopping-off place. All had to learn to pronounce the name of the place, which means "long lake" in Iroquois. It's "Skinny-ata-less."

Situated in the center of town, the Sherwood enjoys a commanding view of the lake and is just across the street from the town pier and a small park. The inn is a popular eatery, even for those not staying overnight in one of the fifteen guest rooms filled with antiques.

If you are visiting during the summer months you can enjoy a unique "mail boat" cruise around the glistening blue lake while the Mid-Lakes Navigation Co. delivers the mail to lakeside residents. There are also dinner cruises and longer cruises along the Erie Barge Canal.

There is an air of elegance, prosperity, and genteel refinement about Skaneateles. Sunday afternoon polo games are played here during the summer. The public is invited to come and watch the sport of kings. Interest in polo is on the rise in the United States. It has been called the fastest game in the world. The word *polo* is derived from the Tibetan word *pulu*, meaning "ball." The game's exact origin is not known, but it was played in Persia more than 1,200 years ago, and the Chinese claim their ancestors took part in polo games 1,000 years before the birth of Christ.

The Skaneateles polo field is on the west shore of the lake, just a short distance from the village center. The games are considered a time for family fun. There are no bleachers, so spectators may bring their own seats or sit on the grass. Many families plan picnics either before or after the game. For those unfamiliar with the rules of the game, the Skaneateles Polo Club publishes *Polo Sundays*. Even if you don't know anything about the game, this is an opportunity to see handsome horses galloping by while watching the shimmering lake below.

Genesee Street (US 20), the village's Main Street, is lined with quaint shops and well-preserved, elegant nineteenth-century homes. Just off Genesee is Doug's Fish Fry, which advertises, "Eat where the local folks eat." Fish is flown in fresh each day from Boston. There is no soft music, panoramic views, or elegant atmosphere, but as Doug says "We don't charge you for it, either." Down Genesee is the Krebs, which has welcomed diners since 1899. It features a back-to-the-farm, plate-passing pigout with all kinds of side dishes and down-home main dishes of fried chicken, ham, and beef.

For more than a century, Skaneateles was known as the teasel capital of the country. Farmers throughout the area grew the plant with a burr head. It was then cut and trimmed and used in the manufacture of woolen cloth to raise the nap of the wool. Teasels were the lucrative crop of the area from 1833 to the end of World War II. The only remnants of the once thriving industry can be found in names such as Teasel Lane and the Teasel Card & Gift Shop, a cute shop that sells gift items but no teasels.

From Skaneateles you could take State 41 along the east side of the lake to the bottom of the lake and then up State 41A and back to US 20. Or you could travel west on US 20 for seven miles to Auburn. This is a city whose history speaks to the rise and decline of the industrial northeast. Just north of Owasco Lake, waterpower attracted Auburn's first settlers.

It's also known as the home of William H. Seward, who is noted for spearheading the purchase of Alaska from the Russians in 1867 while serving as secretary of state under Johnson. The banks and schools are closed in Alaska every year on the last Monday in March in honor of Seward. His home attracts Alaskan visitors, who travel 6,000 miles to see where the statesman slept, worked, and lived.

Seward thought he would become president, but the Republicans didn't nominate him in 1860, opting instead for Abraham Lincoln. They feared Seward was too radical and would get the country into a civil war. Seward had served as state senator, governor, and United States senator.

Seward's home was built in 1816 by his father-in-law and law partner, Judge Elijah Miller. Among those who worked on its construction and built the fireplace mantel in the parlor was Brigham Young, then a sixteen-year-old journeyman painter and carpenter, who later became head of the Mormon Church. Seward lived here from the time of his marriage in 1824 until 1872, when he died on the couch in the north library. After his death, the home was occupied by his son and then his grandson. After his grandson's death in 1951, the house was given to a foundation as a memorial to his famous grandfather. As a result, the home is chock full of Seward's possessions, just as when he lived here.

During President Andrew Johnson's term Seward negotiated the purchase of Alaska with the nation's defense in mind, even though Americans laughed at the place they called "Seward's Folly" or "Seward's Icebox." Of course, he could not have foreseen the riches in gold, oil, furs, and other natural resources the nation has reaped from the forty-ninth state. The purchase occurred at four o'clock in the morning of March 30, 1867, when Seward and Russian Minister Edward Stoeckl signed the treaty turning "Russian America" over to the United States. The event was immortalized in oil by Emanuel Leutze, the artist who is best known for his *Washington Crossing the Delaware. The Signing of the Alaska Treaty* dominates the second floor stairwell of Seward's home, called the diplomatic gallery.

The gallery comprises Seward's collection of 132 prints and photographs of world leaders he met on diplomatic missions around the globe. It is a virtual who's-who of mid-nineteenth-century rulers. In addition to the gallery, the second floor holds a room converted for the display of Civil War relics and documents, including handwritten letters from Abraham Lincoln to Seward. Also exhibited is a military uniform, which, although small in size, was a perfect fit for the slightly built, five-foot-four-inch Seward.

Seward brought back many treasures from his diplomatic journeys to far-off places, as well as collecting gifts from foreign guests visiting Washington. He was prepared for entertaining large crowds with a sixty-place set of china, a gift of Prince Napolean Joseph Charles Paul Bonaparte, the French emperor's nephew. There are reminders of Alaska everywhere, including an Alaskan kayak and rare armor worn by Alaskan Indians.

Just about a mile from Seward's South Street house is another spot worth a visit—the Willard Memorial Chapel on Nelson, which is the only complete and unaltered Tiffany chapel known to exist. The chapel and the adjoining Welch Memorial Building are all that remain of the Auburn Theological Seminary. For generations from 1818 to 1939, it was home to Presbyterian scholars, missionaries, and ministers. Then it moved to New York City to become affiliated with Union Theological Seminary. The interior of the chapel, which seats

250, was designed and handcrafted entirely by the Tiffany Glass and Decorating Co. of New York.

Just south of Auburn is Owasco Lake. The Iroquois Indian Trail traversed the shore of the lake. Take State 38 south, which hugs the west shore of the fourteen-mile-long lake. The Springside Inn, just a mile down the lake, is a large clapboard Victorian house that has been welcoming travelers for generations.

The origins of the inn overlooking Lake Owasco go back to 1851 and a Dutch Reform pastor who opened a boys' school in his three-story home, hoping to help his pupils "avoid the evils necessarily attendant upon large and promiscuous assemblages of the young." The pastor went on to missionary

The Springside Inn at Lake Owasco

work in Japan and his home passed through several hands until in 1919 it was converted to a summer resort. Twenty years later, it was turned into a year-round inn. The Sunday brunch attracts area residents from miles around for the bountiful food, including the house specialties—cheese soufflé and make-your-own sundaes.

If you wish to continue down State 38 to the foot of the lake, you'll find a spacious park—Emerson Park—with a swimming beach, lawns, picnic facilities, and playgrounds. The park includes a pavilion, where the Syracuse Symphony plays free summer concerts, a dance hall, and bathhouses.

From Auburn, it's just about ten miles west to another sparkling Finger Lake—Cayuga Lake.

In the Area

All numbers are in area code 315.

Sainte Marie Among the Iroquois (Liverpool): 453-6767

Onondaga Lake Park (Liverpool): 451-PARK

Salt Museum (Liverpool): 453-6715

The Sherwood Inn (Skaneateles): 685-3405

Mid-Lake Navigation Co., Ltd. (Skaneateles): 685-8500

Doug's Fish Fry (Skaneateles): 685-3288

The Krebs (Skaneateles): 685-5714

The William Seward House (Auburn): 252-1283

Willard Memorial Chapel (Auburn): 252-0339

Springside Inn (Auburn): 252-7247

Emerson Park (Auburn): 253-5611

9 ~

Geneva

From Rochester and points west: Take I-390 south to Bath. Take State 54 north to Hammondsport. From New York City take State 17 west to State 54 north to Hammondsport.

Highlights: *Heart of Finger Lakes wine region, beautiful scenery, aviation museum, and birthplace of Glenn Curtiss.*

Wineries galore grace the slopes of Keuka Lake and Seneca Lake. There are scenic vistas from every hill or turn of the road. Hammondsport, the birthplace of grape culture in the Finger Lakes wine region, is also the birthplace of aviation pioneer Glenn Curtiss and is home to a newly expanded museum in his honor. The tour begins in Hammondsport on Keuka Lake and ends in Watkins Glen on Seneca Lake. This could be a day trip, but depending on how many wineries you visit and other stops you make, consider an overnight in one of the area's elegant and unique inns.

The village of Hammondsport is known as the birthplace of Finger Lakes wineries. It was 1829 when the Reverend William Bostwick transplanted Isabella and Catawba grapevines from the Hudson Valley to his rectory at St. James Episcopal Church. He wanted to make sacramental wine for his parishioners. The grapes flourished and news of Bostwick's success spread rapidly among nearby farmers.

These farmers discovered that the origins of the Finger Lakes led to ideal conditions for growing grapes. Iroquois legend has it that the Finger Lakes region was formed when the Great Spirit placed his hand in blessing on this favored land. The geologists' explanation is more prosaic: The lakes were created when Ice Age glaciers retreated about a million years ago. The intense pressure of those ice masses created the long, narrow lakes lying side by side, the deep gorges with rushing falls, and the wide, fertile valleys that extend south for miles. These features are found nowhere else in the world.

The moving ice masses deposited a shallow layer of topsoil on sloping shale beds above the lakes, providing the drainage crucial for grape growing. Grapevines don't like having "wet feet." The glaciers also furnished the vineyards with protection from the region's sometimes fickle climate. The deep lakes retain their summer warmth in the fall and their winter cold in the spring, moderating the temperature along their shores.

In 1860, thirteen Hammondsport businessmen purchased land about two miles south of their town and resolved to form a company "for the production and manufacture of native wine." Built on a slope overlooking Pleasant Valley, just south of town, the Hammondsport and Pleasant Valley Wine Company became the first commercial winery to open in the region.

The growth of wineries created new jobs in the sleepy town of Hammondsport and a young carpenter named Walter

Taylor arrived to make barrels for the wineries. During his first years in Hammondsport he made his home in a grape shanty a few miles north of town. Impressed by the success of his employers, Taylor began planting grapevines and making wine himself. His wine was an immediate success and within three years he gave up making barrels and launched his own winery. In time, his winery would become the largest in the Finger Lakes region.

The Taylor Winery visitors center is the largest and most elaborate winery operation. Take State 54 from Bath north for

Grapes ready for harvest in the Finger Lakes

approximately five miles and turn left at Pleasant Valley. Follow the signs to the visitors center. Many of the yellow mansard-roofed buildings date back to the Civil War era and the beginnings of winemaking in the region.

At the entrance to the center is a movie theater built in a former wine tank. Where 35,000 gallons of wine once fermented, now forty people view films on the history of the wineries. All wines made by Taylor, Great Western, and Gold Seal may be sampled at a sixty-six-foot horseshoe bar. Just beyond is the area's largest winery retail shop. The hour-long tour is one of the most complete in the region. During the fall harvest season, visitors start their tour with a stop at a nearby pressing building. It's hard to match a clear fall day in a vineyard, especially a vineyard with a view of Keuka Lake.

The twenty-two-mile-long Keuka Lake is one of the loveliest in the Finger Lakes region and the only one shaped like a Y. Nineteenth-century settlers called the lake Crooked Lake and "the Lady of the Lakes." Even the wines taste better when you are tasting within sight of the lake. For the best view of the lake and the vineyards along the hillsides, take a ride on the *Keuka Maid*, which hosts lunch and dinner cruises from May to October.

Just outside Hammondsport on State 54 is the newly expanded Glenn Curtiss Museum, now housed in a former Gold Seal wine warehouse. Born in the village in 1878, Glenn Curtiss grew up fascinated with mechanics and speed. Those loves led to his involvement with bicycles, then motorcycles, and finally airplanes. In 1907, Dr. Alexander Graham Bell, of telephone fame, formed the Aerial Experiment Association with Curtiss as a director, and the fame of Hammondsport as the aviation center of the country began.

Through the years, Curtiss piled up achievements and broke records. He held the first publicly witnessed flight in America, the June Bug flight of 1908; designed and built the world's fastest plane, which was clocked at 46 mph in 1909; piloted the first long distance flight, a full 150 miles from Albany to New York City in 1910; gave the first demonstration of aerial bombing; and designed the first plane purchased by the United States Navy. He was the holder of United States pilot's license number one. The Curtiss Museum chronicles the early days and development of aviation and the contributions of Curtiss.

Between tastings and museum visits, it's a pleasure to walk around Hammondsport's town square eating ice cream from the Crooked Lake Ice Cream Company. The Reverend Bostwick's St. James Episcopal Church is here. Just off the square is Opera House Antiques, a group shop with fifteen dealers offering an array of antiques, jewelry, art works, and other collectibles.

From the village take State 76 north. Just a mile outside town is the famed Bully Hill Winery and the Greyton H. Taylor Wine Museum. Walter S. Taylor named the museum in honor of his father, one of the sons of the founder of the Taylor Wine Co. Walter S. Taylor is known throughout the wine world for his court battles with the Coca-Cola Co. (which owned Taylor Wine Co. at the time) over the use of his name on Bully Hill Wines. Although Walter S., as he is now known, lost the court battles, he won in the court of public opinion. The world press flocked to Bully Hill after Taylor was forbidden to use his name on his wines. Walter S. turned the entire affair into a public-relations bonanza. Bully Hill offers tours and tastings.

The museum displays artifacts from the long history of winemaking in the region. It occupies century-old buildings that once served as the original production plant for Taylor wines. One building houses a collection of wine bottles dating back more than 100 years, including some owned by President Buchanan. The Bully Hill Restaurant stresses fresh ingredients served in a splendid setting overlooking the vineyards and the deep blue lake. Spreading in all directions is a magnificent sweep of vineyards circling the lake. On a clear day, an azure slice of Seneca Lake, some forty miles away, may be glimpsed through the hills. Bully Hill operates a bed and breakfast just down the road.

For other wineries follow the Keuka Winery Route, distinguished by its red-and-white signs. Although State 54A hugs the lake, the higher State 76 offers some of the most scenic vantage points in all the Finger Lakes and most of the wineries can be reached from this route.

Back on State 54A follow the lake to Branchport. Just beyond Branchport is Keuka Lake State Park, which boasts stunning views of the lake and vineyards. Trails take hikers among the trees and hills. From the park, continue along State 54A. You will be driving across the middle of the Y.

The next vantage point and stop is Bluff Point. Between East Bluff Drive and Sky Line Drive, look for a seven-foot, green iron fence. Behind the fence is the Little Chapel on the Mount, maintained by the Rochester Episcopal Diocese. The grounds are open during the summer and church services are held on Sunday mornings. The stone chapel was built by Captain Paul Garrett, America's first wine magnate, as a memorial to his fourth son, who died at age sixteen.

Just beyond Bluff Point is Keuka College, a lovely campus on the lake. Stop for a look at Norton Chapel, with its inspiring mosaic-glass windows designed by Gabriel Loire, distinguished artist of Chartres, France. The chapel sits on the edge of the lake and is designed on the plan of a Latin cross.

Two miles down State 54A look for the sign for Apple Barrel Orchards, which advertises "Bushels of Good Health." During the apple picking season in late summer and early fall, the orchards are open for picking and for apple purchases by the bushel or bag. From the orchards there's a superb view of Keuka Lake below—it's worth a visit for the view alone.

State 54A continues into Penn Yan, the world's largest producer of buckwheat products. Tours of Birkett Mills are given during the Annual Buckwheat Harvest Festival during the last weekend in September.

The town still remembers Jemina Wilkinson, the Universal Publick Friend. She led one of the many religious groups that looked for a new Eden in western New York in the early 1800s. One day she gathered her followers by the shore of Keuka Lake and asked them if they believed she could walk on water. They believed, but instead of giving them the demonstration they wanted, she announced that if they believed in her power, then she need not demonstrate it.

If you are traveling on a Saturday from May through December take a detour south from Penn Yan on State 14A to the Windmill Farm and Craft Market. More than 150 vendors offer farm-fresh foods, plants, crafts, antiques, quilts, cheeses, baked goods, Mennonite specialities, and more.

Going north on State 14A from Penn Yan, you will see road signs with a horse and buggy on them—indicating a Mennonite community in the area. You may spot a horse and black buggy clip-clopping down the road. Off State 14A on the side roads are Mennonite farms—many selling handcrafted furniture, quilts, and baked goods from roadside stands. Look for signs tacked to poles along the roads.

Continue on into Geneva, which is aptly named after the town on the shores of Lake Geneva in Switzerland. Geneva is on the northern tip of Seneca Lake, the self-proclaimed "Lake Trout Capital of the World." It is home to the National Lake Trout Derby held on Memorial Day weekend. With a depth of 650 feet, it is the deepest of the Finger Lakes.

There is an air of elegance and solid permanence about Geneva, which was one of the earliest settlements in this part of the state. In 1794, Charles Williamson arrived in town as manager of the Pulteney Estate, lands that included nearly all of Geneva and the Genesee region to the west. He laid out the main streets of Geneva and did extensive publicizing of the area, attracting wealthy gentlemen from Virginia and Maryland.

During the nineteenth century, Geneva prospered and became a thriving community, a place where many residents "enjoyed, rather than made, their fortune." The legacy of early Geneva lies in the variety and quality of its buildings. Pick up a self-guided walking tour guide to South Main Street at 543 Main Street—the Prouty-Chew House, now owned by the Geneva Historical Society. The city's South Main Street has been proclaimed "the most beautiful street in America." Geneva is the home of Hobart and William Smith colleges. It has been a college town since 1822, when Bishop Hobart founded Geneva College, which in 1851 became Hobart College.

Until 1872 there was an affiliated Geneva Medical College. The medical college is famous for having awarded in 1849 the first American medical degree to a woman, Elizabeth Blackwell. Born in England, she overcame incredible odds to accomplish her dream of becoming a physician. Her fellow students thought her application was a hoax and seemed to them "against all decency of the time." The Elizabeth Blackwell Gallery, located in the Demarest Library on the campus, is open to visitors.

The town echoes with the lives of prosperous nineteenth-century merchants and farmers, who built stately Federal, Greek Revival, Gothic, and Italianate homes.

Geneva is also known for two of the state's most special and unique inns. Just past the South Main Street Historic District on State 14S is a 1911 Italianate villa built by malt tycoon Bryon Nester. It was modeled after the Villa Lancel-lotti, a sixteenth-century villa in Frascati, near Rome. It has served as a Capuchin monastery, an apartment complex, and since 1981, a small, elegant resort with twenty-nine luxurious suites.

Geneva-on-the-Lake is one of the state's most beautiful inns. It has formal hedged gardens and a seventy-foot swimming pool overlooking the lake. The pool is surrounded by Roman columns and the lawns are dotted with reproductions of classical statuary, including Venus de Milo, Hermes, and the Esquiline Venus. The inn was renovated by the Schickel family of Ithaca. One suite has two bedrooms, two fireplaces, a canopied bed, a balcony overlooking the lake, and a kitchen. My favorite is the Library Suite, with floor-to-ceiling bookcases stocked with Schickel family books, a wood-burning fireplace and carved stone mantel, and tall windows opening out to the garden and lake.

Less than a mile down the road is the Belhurst Castle. In 1885 Carrie Harron Collins, a newly married socialite from Cincinnati, asked Albert W. Fuller, a favorite architect of the day, to design a castle complete with turrets. He and fifty craftsmen labored six days a week for four years to create her fantasy, which boasts turrets, gargoyles, and decorative terra cotta. She and her husband and twenty-two servants lived in the Romanesque mansion for nearly forty years. It is surrounded by ancient firs and white oaks and set among twenty-five acres of lawns and gardens sloping down to Seneca Lake.

Soon after Mrs. Collins's death, the home was acquired by Red Dwyer, a gambler and colorful character who operated it as a speakeasy with rooms for some of his hard-up buddies. Since 1975, it has been transformed into an inn with twelve rooms and suites. The castle sports carved oak, cherry, and mahogany, and more stained glass than many churches. Many rooms have gas-fired fireplaces. A silver spigot on the second-floor landing dispenses Finger Lakes wine to inn guests. Mrs. Collins's bedroom is one of the inn's suites. An ornately carved 1810 mahogany four-poster bed is so high that guests need a stool to get into bed. Upstairs, the Victorian ballroom with eighteen-foot ceilings has been converted into the Tower Suite with a Finnish sauna and a lookout in the turret's attic. You'll see a large living room and an equally enormous bedroom.

Three miles outside town on State 96A overlooking Seneca Lake is Rose Hill, built in 1839 and restored to its original elegance. Now on the National Register of Historic Places, its twenty-one rooms are furnished in Empire style. It has been called "one of the finest Greek Revival houses in the United States" and is open from May to October as a house museum.

Continue south on Rt 96A along the east side of Seneca Lake. Follow the signs for the Seneca Lake Wine Trail. The first stop and a perfect choice for lunch, dinner, or brunch on Sundays is Wagner Vineyards, home of the Ginny Lee Cafe. Named after Bill Wagner's granddaughter, the cafe is an extension of the tasting and tour and overlooks the vineyards and deep blue lake. During the warm weather, the outside deck is the most popular spot for a meal. Musical evenings are planned during the summer.

The next stop is Poplar Ridge Vineyards, whose owner, David Bagley, believes there is too much hocus-pocus in the wine industry. This is a medium-size farm winery where Mr. Bagley presides over every aspect of the winery and often serves wines at the tastings. "Wine is not a religion or cult or something to intimidate your neighbor with," he says.

A few miles farther down Seneca Lake is Hazlitt 1852 Vineyards, one of the newer wineries. Jerry Hazlitt's family established the main farm in 1852, and he made wines for his friends for years before opening the winery.

Continue south on State 414 to Watkins Glen on the southern end of the thirty-eight-mile-long Seneca Lake. The big attraction here is a spectacular gorge that traces its origins back 10,000 years to the end of the Ice Age. The chasm forms the heart of Watkins Glen State Park. The best way to experience the beauty of the glen is to hike the gorge trail, which is over one-and-a-half miles long and has over 800 stone steps. It is not a difficult walk, but the footing can get slippery. The glen drops about 700 feet in two miles and is highlighted by rock formations and eighteen waterfalls. In places you will walk behind some of the waterfalls and at some points you will actually be standing on the floor of an ancient sea. Cliffs rise 200 feet above the stream; a 165-foot-high bridge spans the glen, which is lighted at night.

You'll find campsites in the park, and in the evening Timespell, a forty-five-minute dramatic sound and laser-light show, traces the natural and human history of the gorge. The stirring voice of the narrator says, "We are about to leave human time altogether and go far, far back into the geologic past . . . to a time when the earth was young—over four-and-a-half billion years ago."

Watkins Glen is also known as "the Home of American Road Racing." Road races are no longer held on the village streets, but on the hills above the village at the newly revitalized Watkins Glen International Racing Circuit. Don't leave Seneca Lake without seeing the lake from the water. Captain Bill's Seneca Lake Cruises offers sightseeing and lunch and dinner cruises.

In the Area

Taylor Winery Visitors Center (Hammondsport):
607-569-6292

Keuka Maid (Hammondsport): 607-569-2628

Glenn H. Curtiss Museum of Local History
(Hammondsport): 607-569-2160

Opera House Antiques (Hammondsport): 607-569-3525

Greyton H. Taylor Wine Museum (Hammondsport):
607-868-4814

Bully Hill Restaurant (Hammondsport): 607-868-3490

Bully Hill Winery (Hammondsport): 607-868-3610

Keuka Lake State Park (Branchport): 315-536-3666

Little Chapel on the Mount (Bluff Point): 716-473-2977

Keuka College (Keuka Park): 315-536-4411

Apple Barrel Orchards (Penn Yan): 315-536-6818

Birkett Mills (Penn Yan): 315-536-7434

Windmill Farm & Craft Market (Penn Yan): 315-536-3032

Geneva Historical Society (Geneva): 315-789-5151

Geneva-on-the-Lake (Geneva): 800-3GENEVA or
315-789-7190

Belhurst Castle (Geneva): 315-781-0201

Rose Hill (Geneva): 315-789-3848

Wagner Winery (Lodi): 607-582-6450

Poplar Ridge (Valois): 607-582-6421

Hazlitt 1852 Vineyards (Hector): 607-546-5812

Watkins Glen State Park (Watkins Glen): 607-535-4511

Timespell (Watkins Glen): 607-535-4960

Captain Bill's Seneca Lake Cruises (Watkins Glen):
607-535-4541

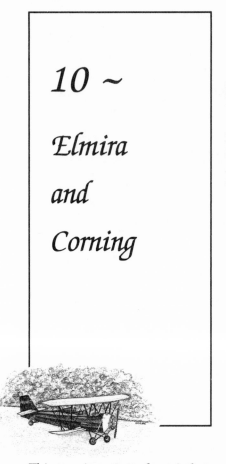

10 ~

Elmira
and
Corning

Take State 17 just east of Elmira, where the tour begins.

Highlights: *Revolutionary War battlefield, Mark Twain's study, National Soaring Museum, Corning Glass Museum.*

This tour is an easy day trip between the Elmira and Corning areas in the south central section of the state. It begins at the Newton Battlefield Reservation, a Revolutionary War battlefield, and continues west with stops at Mark Twain's study, the National Soaring Museum, the Corning Glass Museum, and other Corning attractions. It would be a good side trip if you are exploring the Finger Lakes to the north.

Begin at the Newtown Battlefield Reservation off State 17 and Lowman Road, about five miles east of Elmira. It was the spring of 1779 when Major General John Sullivan, under the command of George Washington, began preparations for a military foray into central New York, seeking to halt the Indian attacks that were plaguing the American forces.

Washington ordered General Sullivan to "lay waste all the settlements around so that the country may not only be overrun but destroyed." Sullivan vigorously carried out Washington's orders and destroyed forty-one settlements, including what is now Geneva, then a large village of fifty houses.

The reservation marks the location of a decisive victory for Sullivan over a large force of Indians and Tories. Not far from the actual battlefield is a monument commemorating this confrontation on August 29, 1779. Sullivan Hill is a part of a reservation that is also a state park with facilities for overnight campers.

Samuel Clemens, aka Mark Twain, spent more than twenty summers in the Elmira area and wrote many of his classics, including *The Adventures of Huckleberry Finn*, here. His wife, Olivia Langdon, grew up in the area, and Clemens loved the Chemung Valley, which he called "a foretaste of heaven." The spot Twain found to write his immortal works was Quarry Farm on East Hill outside Elmira. This "perfect place" was built there for him in 1874 by his wife's sister, Mrs. Theodore Crane.

Twain described it as "the loveliest study you ever saw. It is octagonal in shape with a peaked roof, each space filled with a spacious window and it sits perched in complete isolation on the very top of an elevation that commands leagues of valleys and city and retreating ranges of blue hills." In 1955, the study was moved to the campus of Elmira College, where it sits today, complete with a typewriter like Twain's. He was one of the first to submit a typed manuscript to a publisher.

"I think Elmira was good for Twain," says Robert Jerome, a local Twain expert. "As a result of Elmira, Twain developed as a writer." Jerome, who coauthored *Mark Twain in Elmira* with Dr. Herbert A. Wisbey, Jr., recalled: "Sam Clemens came here first for the health-giving air and the atmosphere, which was great for the children and great for Livy (his wife)." Twain wrote to people about Elmira saying: "I produced more today than I ever could anywhere else."

Twain and his family are buried in Woodlawn City Cemetery in Elmira. There is a monument to Twain and Ossip Gabrilowitsch, Twain's son-in-law, that contains likenesses of

Mark Twain's study resembles a Mississippi riverboat pilothouse

Twain and Gabrilowitsch on a shaft twelve feet high (or two fathoms), the "Mark Twain" of Mississippi riverboats.

During the summer, Twain lovers can take a short detour north on State 14 to the Elmira College Domes, where "America's Tribute to Mark Twain," a musical drama, is performed Tuesdays through Sundays.The Elmira area is known as the "Soaring Capital of America," and the area's hills and valleys present ideal airplane soaring and gliding conditions. It has been known as the soaring capital since the first National Soaring Contest was held in 1930 on a mountaintop south of Elmira. Take State 352 west to Harris Hill Road and the National Soaring Museum. It's midway between Elmira and Corning.

Everyone wants to know the difference between gliding and soaring. The Soaring Society of America explains: "Gliding is coasting downhill on an inclined plane of air; soaring is maintaining or gaining altitude in upcurrents of air. Upcurrents occur for a variety of reasons, the most common being uneven heating of the ground by the sun which results in rising columns or bubbles of hot air called thermals."

The National Soaring Museum displays more than a dozen fully assembled historic gliders and sailplanes, as well as artifacts pertaining to motorless flight. You can sit in a simulator cockpit to experience the soaring sensation. For the real thing, take a sailplane ride at the adjacent glider field or just watch the sailplanes perform.

From the museum take State 17 into Corning. Although Corning has been known as the City of Glass for more than a century, it took a hurricane and a flood to transform this town into a thriving tourist attraction.

After the 1972 floodwaters receded, the wondrous Corning Museum of Glass was completely rebuilt, and the four-block-long Market Street, downtown Corning's main thoroughfare, was restored and recognized as the historic jewel that it is. These nineteenth-century buildings are now listed with the National Register of Historic Places.

The Corning Glass Center first opened in 1951 to mark the 100th birthday of Corning Glass Works. One of Corning's earliest major projects was the production of bulbs for electric lights invented by Thomas Alva Edison. The museum houses the world's largest collection of glass objects—more than 22,000 in all—and now attracts over half a million visitors yearly. The present building, designed by architect Gunnar Birkerts, opened in 1980 and is remarkable in its ability both to showcase the glass and to provide for the comfort of visitors.

Guided tours through the museum encompass thirty-five centuries of man's experience with glass, starting with such fascinating creations as the head of Amenhotep II, the earliest known portrait in glass, and the Omphalos Bowl from Persia, dating from 500–400 B.C. Visitors may even gently touch the bottom of a glass bottle found among the remains in a 2,000-year-old Roman tomb.

The glass collection ranges from weapons chipped from volcanic glass by prehistoric people to hand-formed glass created by contemporary artists.

Connected to the museum is the Hall of Science and Industry, which sets out to show that learning about glass can be both educational and fun. Films, push-button displays, and demonstrations are designed to show the versatility of glass. You can watch a glass magician pound a nail with a glass hammer, stretch the stem of a wineglass six feet by heating the glass, and see a still-frozen Popsicle wrapped in an insulated glass bag after it has been baked in a hot oven. Kids will enjoy scaling the fiberglass climbing unit, which has lots of compartments to hide in. Watch the glass artisan transform glass rods into tiny animals.

A highlight of the tour is the third stop on the glass-center tour—the Steuben Glass Factory. Steuben Glass was founded in 1903 by Frederick Carder, who spent nearly eighty of his 100 years designing and making glass in Corning. Carder's glass works are on display in the Museum of Glass and the nearby Rockwell Museum.

A seventeenth-century Florentine, Antonio Neri, wrote the first book about glassmaking. "Glass," he wrote, "is more gentle, graceful and noble than any metal, and its use is more delightful, polite and sightly than any other material . . . known to the world." For 3,500 years, glass has been made in the same way, and since 1676, the finest glass, called crystal, has been made by adding lead.

Steuben strives to make the finest glass objects in the world. These works of art are regularly given by U.S. presidents to heads of state all over the world. Steuben glass pieces are in the finest glass collections throughout the world. To make its glass, Steuben buys the world's purest sand from an area in Africa. Visitors watch glass come to life under the skilled hands of artists. The glass is red hot and flowing like honey before it becomes one of the unique Steuben creations. Visitors may also see the grinding, polishing, inspecting, and engraving operations.

During the summer, double-decker buses provide free transportation between the glass center and historic Market Street. After a decade-long restoration effort, the street includes fine examples of Victorian-style brick and terra cotta architecture.

The Rockwell Museum, which houses the largest collection of western art east of the Mississippi, makes its home in the former city hall. The museum houses the collection of long-time Corning residents, Robert and Hertha Rockwell, featuring extensive collections of antique guns and Navajo rugs, antique toys, and the magnificent Carder glass.

The Wine Center, in the old Baron Steuben Hotel, offers a series of educational exhibits focusing on the history and production of wine. The development of the cork stopper in the eighteenth century revolutionized winemaking. Wine-making in the United States has had a considerable history, even though winemakers had to contend with the rigors of Prohibition.

You will learn to properly open and serve a bottle of what Louis Pasteur called "the most hygienic and faithful of beverages." In the tasting room you can sample wines from fourteen different New York State wineries and purchase your favorites. If your sweet tooth is acting up, stop at the Ice Cream Works on the main floor of the old hotel. With its Tiffany-style lighting, long marble counter, and lace curtains, the Victorian ambience is abundant and the ice cream and sauces are overflowing and positively sinful. Properly refreshed, you are ready to continue your journey.

In the Area

All numbers are in area code 607.

Newton Battlefield Reservation (Elmira): 732-1096

Elmira College (Elmira): 735-1800

America's Tribute to Mark Twain (Elmira): 732-2152

National Soaring Museum (Elmira): 734-3128

Corning Glass Center (Corning): 974-8271

Rockwell Museum (Corning): 937-5386

Rockwell's Department Store (Corning): 962-7807

The Wine Center (Corning): 962-6072

Ice Cream Works (Corning): 962-8481

11 ~

Aurora:
US 20A

From Buffalo and points east and west: Take the New York Thruway to State 400 to East Aurora, twenty miles southeast of Buffalo.

Highlights: *Roycroft campus, Millard Fillmore's home, top dairy farming areas, Letchworth State Park, Indian museum, air show, Genesee Country Museum.*

The length of this tour depends on your interests. While it is possible to make the drive, which is only about seventy-five miles from East Aurora to Mumford, in a day, it is best to plan for a weekend tour, especially if you wish to enjoy the village, the park, and the Genesee Country Museum. If you are planning to attend the air show in Geneseo, which is held annually in mid-August, count on spending at least half a day there. You can also easily spend a half day or longer at the Genesee Country Museum.

East Aurora retains much of its nineteenth-century flavor. Large, Victorian-style houses line the village streets. During the spring, summer, and fall a thriving farmer's market offers fresh-from-the-farm products every Wednesday and Saturday morning at the Aurora Village Shopping Center.

The Globe Hotel on Main Street has been welcoming diners since 1824. The third-floor dance hall was added more than 100 years ago. Local lore has it that area residents driving livestock to Buffalo for sale would stop at the Globe for refreshment while the animals freely roamed Main Street.

It's easy to imagine a young Millard Fillmore walking across Main Street from his law office to meet with the town leaders at the Globe. Millard Fillmore, the country's thirteenth president, built the Greek Revival cottage at 24 Shearer Avenue for his bride, Abigail.

He began his law career in East Aurora and his influence still can be found in western New York. He was a founder of the University of Buffalo and the historical society. Fillmore's home has been restored and includes some original Fillmore furnishings, such as his desk and the volumes of law books in his tiny office. Climb the steep and narrow staircase to the second floor, where some of Fillmore's white linen shirts are displayed on his bed. Next door is a child's playroom, where it is believed that Fillmore's son, Millard Powers Fillmore, was born.

Throughout history, Fillmore's reputation has suffered much cruel ribbing. He is one of just a handful of presidents who were never elected to the office, and there are those who say that Fillmore's most noteworthy accomplishment was the installation of the White House's first bathtub. But in his home in East Aurora, guides speak with pride about Fillmore and about his Compromise of 1850, which delayed the start of the Civil War for ten years.

Paintings of Fillmore show a tall and handsome man. It was reported that Queen Victoria called him "the most handsome man in the world." The house is open to the public as a museum. The grounds include a rose garden and a period herb garden. You'll see a sleigh and a carriage in the barn.

But it was Elbert Hubbard, "the sage of East Aurora," who brought the most fame to the village. The successful soap-company-executive-turned-philosopher-and-writer founded the Roycroft Movement in 1895. At its peak there were more than 500 printers, coppersmiths, furnituremakers, silver-smiths, potters, artists, and innkeepers at Roycroft. The name came from Samuel and Thomas Roycroft, seventeenth-century English bookbinders, or, some say, from royal craft, meaning "quality distinguished as suitable for the royal household."

The complex of ten buildings was known nationally as a community of artisans and devotees of the arts-and-crafts movement. The buildings were listed on the National Register of Historic Places in 1974. Visitors such as Thomas Edison, Henry Ford, Clarence Darrow, Clara Barton, and Booker T. Washington traveled to East Aurora to be inspired by Hub-bard and his philosophy, which was devoted to "Better art, better work and a better and more reasonable way of living."

An 1896 issue of his magazine, *The Philistine*, carried this general invitation: "All good Philistines . . . welcome to seats at the table and a place to sleep—of course without charge. All men and women, however, who remain over one night are expected to work for the public good at least two hours a day. There is type setting, proof reading, copying and addressing wrappers to do, besides taking care of the Roycroft Baby (lim-ited edition—de luxe copy), cooking, washing, and then there is a good big wood pile."

It was soon apparent that this was no way to run a house-hold, and the Roycroft Inn was created out of several build-ings in 1903. The rooms were not numbered, but named: Socrates, Edison, William Morris, Brahms, Susan B. Anthony. Rates were instituted—25 cents a meal and 50 cents a night.

The massive front door is engraved with the motto: "Produce Great People, the Rest Follows." The inn has been closed for the past couple of years and is currently undergoing restoration.

Across the street, other campus buildings house a gift shop filled with locally made crafts, original and new Roycroft books, and interior design and bridal studios. You'll find a pottery shop, antique shop, silversmith, campus printshop, and an art gallery. The stone chapel (built from stones from neighboring farms) now houses the Aurora Town Hall and the Aurora Town Museum. Down the street on Oakwood Avenue is the Elbert Hubbard Museum, which has an important collection of Roycroft and Hubbard materials.

Hubbard and his wife, Alice, died in the sinking of the passenger liner *Lusitania* by a German U-boat on May 7, 1915. The Roycroft campus continued to thrive under the guidance of his son, Elbert II, until the Depression caused the closing in 1938. Today, an air of revival permeates the campus and Hubbard's creativity and philosophy are still attracting visitors.

In keeping with the theme of an earlier, simpler time, stop at Vidler's 5 & 10 on Main Street. It's easy to spot with the distinctive red-and-white awning. The store is housed in a 100-year-old building with sprawling additions. It is much as it was when it opened in 1930, with its uneven wooden floors, old, ornate brass cash registers, original popcorn maker offering popcorn for a dime, and a tremendous variety of merchandise—even some items for a nickel or a dime—and a large selection of Fisher-Price toys. The world headquarters of the well-known toy company, founded in 1930, is just two blocks away.

In honor of the Fisher-Price connection, East Aurora bills itself as "Toy Town U.S.A." and celebrates toys and children of all ages each summer with its ToyFest. Held during the last weekend in August, the celebration includes parades, a show and sale of antique toys, concerts, and a host of child-related activities. A Toy Town Museum has been created on Main Street, featuring antique toys. Every year a limited edition commemorative toy is created in honor of the festival.

Just down Main Street, stop at Baker Memorial Church. Built in 1928, it features seventeen windows created by the designers and artisans of the famed Tiffany Studios. Four bear the signature of Louis Comfort Tiffany.

East Aurora was known as the trotting capital of the world in the 1880s, a heritage that is still evident today in the numbers of pleasure riders and stables in the community. That heritage is remembered each summer the last weekend in July with Racing and Reunion Day, which features a competitive carriage drive and marathon sponsored by the East Aurora Driving Society. During the carriage marathon, beautifully restored period carriages are driven through village streets.

The village was the home of the Hamlin Village Farm, which produced many championship trotters. The farm was founded in 1855, with its main barn located on what is now Hamlin Avenue. In 1882 the farm purchased Mambrino King for $17,000. In 1884 the farm superintendent said that not less than 16,000 people had called in to see the animal who had been judged "the most handsome horse in the world." A historical marker on North Willow Street marks Mambrino King's burial site. The Jewett Farm was known as the world's only one-mile covered racetrack. It was built in 1893 and dismantled in the early twenties. Some of the original buildings can be seen on Grover Road. The village's third major farm was the Ideal Stock Farm, founded by Seymour H. Knox and still occupied today by the Knox family.

If you are hungry, before leaving East Aurora drive south on old State 16 to Blakeley Road. You will see the signs for the Old Orchard Inn, a picture-perfect country restaurant. It started life as a farmhouse in the 1860s and was later a hunting lodge and tearoom. Large stone fireplaces burn warmly in the winter. The expansive grounds feature a duck pond and sweeping views of the countryside. Specialties include old-fashioned chicken fricassee with biscuits and chicken pot pie. Sunday dinners feature turkey, ham, roast pork, and prime rib. You'll find a gift shop in the barn and silo.

A few miles outside town on US 20A in the small community of Wales Center is an old-fashioned country tearoom—the Tea Cozy. Every country road should have a place like this—comfortable and welcoming. The glory of the Tea Cozy is the baked goods and the tea, of course. It is served in bone-china cups from fat little pots with multicolored pastel tea cozies. Light lunches and tea are served here. If you order tea you will receive finger sandwiches, scones, dessert, and a small pot of tea. Dessert here is a production and everything is wonderful. If you have a sweet tooth, this is a most pleasant stop.

Outside of Wales Center, you will find yourself in dairy country. In fact, this is one of the state's largest dairy areas. Farmers here take great pride in their land and farms, many of which have been in the same family for generations. Many farms proudly display their Dairy of Distinction emblems signifying that they have qualified as outstanding operations under a state program. The award looks for farmers who place great stock in cleanliness, upkeep, and beauty as well as well-run operations. These are picture-book farms alongside the rolling hills of US 20A as it traverses Wyoming County.

At Perry Center take State 246 south to State 39 to Portageville and the southern entrance of Letchworth State Park, an easy forty-five-minute drive from East Aurora (not counting stops). It is here that the Genesee River runs fast and deep between towering rock walls. The park, which has been called the "Grand Canyon of the East," includes a seventeen-mile gorge and three major waterfalls. Though Letchworth is much smaller than Arizona's Grand Canyon and is largely unknown outside the state, it is still a spectacular gorge. The park is named after Buffalo industrialist William Pryor Letchworth, who rescued and preserved the area.

He first spotted the area one day while returning from a trip to New York on the Erie Railway. A newsboy came through the cars with handbills touting the upcoming bridge as "the longest and highest wooden bridge in the United States, if not in the world; and one of the grandest views on the Western continent." Letchworth was overcome by the scene. A perfect rainbow arched over the falls. He saw the beauty in spite of the lumber operations that had scarred the river's banks and had all but devastated the area.

He soon set about buying a large house he had seen near the gorge and as much land as he could. Letchworth liked the word *iris*, a synonym for rainbow, and named his estate Glen Iris. He continued to buy land in the valley and eventually had 700 acres and three waterfalls.

Letchworth retired early from business and devoted himself to social reform. His efforts bettered the lives of thousands of Indians, the poor, juvenile delinquents, prisoners, epileptics, the blind, and the mentally ill. In 1906 he deeded his land and home to the state and died four years later at his beloved home. He was an early and ardent conservationist and transformed the once scarred landscape into a place of unspoiled beauty.

He was also determined to preserve the region's rich Indian lore. In 1871 he relocated the last of the Genesee Valley's Seneca council houses near Glen Iris. After months of planning, Letchworth conducted the Last Council of the Genesee to rededicate the Council House on October 1, 1872. No such council had been held for seventy years and none would be held again. He extended invitations to descendants of Indian leaders. Spectators included former president Millard

Fillmore and a descendant of Red Jacket. After the ceremony, the Indians had a surprise for Letchworth—they wanted to adopt him into the Seneca Nation, the highest honor they could give him. In a solemn ceremony they named him Hai-wa-ye-is-ta, "the man who always does the right thing."

Letchworth then had the remains of Mary Jemison—the legendary White Woman of the Genesee—moved from a cemetery in Buffalo to the council-house grounds. As a young girl she had been kidnapped by a Shawnee war party and was later adopted by the Senecas. She lived out her long life as a Seneca squaw in the shadow of the gorge. Letchworth had a statue erected marking Mary Jemison's final resting place. She is depicted with long braided hair and with her baby strapped to her back.

The history of the lands and Letchworth himself is told through a slide show, artifacts, books, and displays in the Pioneer and Indian Museum, a short walk from the inn. The park now comprises 14,350 acres of magnificent scenery, which includes 17 miles of the Genesee River; dramatic cliffs, some of which approach 600 feet in height; three major water-falls, one that's 107 feet high; lush forests, many planted by Letchworth himself; a perfect country inn and restaurant—the Glen Iris Inn, Letchworth's former home; and cabins and campsites.

It's often possible to see the rainbow that so enchanted Letchworth just beyond Middle Falls. Although every season has its special charms, it is hard to find beauty surpassing that of a fine fall day when the colors are at their peak. The Glen Iris is booked two years or more in advance for fall weekends. The park has swimming pools and a stocked trout pond and animals abound. But this is not a preserve; the animals are wild, and the park is open for hunting in the fall.

From Mount Morris at the northern boundary of the park, it's a short drive to Geneseo. This area of the lower

Genesee Valley often echoes with the huntsman's horn and the baying of the foxhounds. Teddy Roosevelt sometimes went riding here with leading local families and with the foxhunt parades down Main Street at the opening meet in late September. The Seneca Indians—Keepers of the Western Door of the Iroquois Six Nations—called the area Gennishey, or "beautiful valley."

Geneseo is home to the National Warplane Museum, which houses a large collection of World War II and Korean conflict-era planes. The museum hosts an annual Wings of Eagles Air Show in mid-August, which attracts hundreds of thousands of airplane enthusiasts to expansive fields in the valley. There's the *Fuddy-Duddy*, the B-17 Flying Fortress, the Avro Lancaster, the B-25, and a host of other vintage planes that fly over the grass fields to the delight of the audience. Before their flights the planes are on display for close-up inspections.

From Geneseo take State 39 north to Avon. From there take State 5 west. Mumford is just off State 5 and is home to the Genesee Country Museum, where the nineteenth century in the Genesee Valley has been re-created. It brings to life the personal dream of John L. Wehle, chairman of the Genesee Brewing Company. The museum opened in 1974 and there are approximately fifty restored buildings in the 125-acre village. The buildings were gathered from thirteen counties of the Genesee Valley and represent various stages in the development of the frontier.

Stuart Bolger, the museum's director, roamed the back roads and small towns and hamlets looking for nineteenth-century buildings. Luck has played a role in his acquisitions. He nearly missed a unique two-story log house, dating from about 1814, that was hidden beneath a skin of twentieth-century clapboard. Its true identity was discovered because the house was situated in the path of a proposed highway.

The octagon house at the Genesee Country Museum

Local archaeologists noticed the log construction and notified the museum. A $1.00 payment was made and the house was hauled away log by log.

The elegant 1870 octagon house was the home of Erastus Hyde, a doctor who also headed the spiritualist colony in nearby Lily Dale. Though it is hard to believe, looking at the handsome home fronting the village green, the Foster-Tufts House was serving as a chicken coop before it was rescued.

The Hosmer Inn was being used as a granary when it was discovered. Built in 1818 by Sylvester Hosmer, the inn was a thriving business near Avon along the Genesee Turnpike. It was cut into four pieces for the move to the museum and today visitors can step back into another time, when men and women dined separately. Accounts written by early travelers praise the food and lodgings of the inn.

Unlike Virginia's famed Williamsburg, the Genesee museum strives to show life of the average person engaged in everyday activities. It also attempts to display an entire century. As at Williamsburg, costumed interpreters are on hand to explain and demonstrate pioneer life. They also perform crafts demonstrations such as spinning, weaving, quilting, and working with pottery and tin. Throughout the season, which runs from May through October, there are special events such as a re-creation of the Battle of Gettysburg, a highland gathering, an antique fire apparatus muster, and a nineteenth-century circus.

Just down the road from the museum is the Genesee Country Inn. While it has no connection with the museum, the stone structure was built by Scotsman Philip Garbutt in 1833 with two-foot-thick walls. It was later used as a home and today is a very special bed-and-breakfast inn with ten rooms. The inn is on six acres with a waterfall and duck pond in the backyard.

In the Area

All numbers are in area code 716.

Globe Hotel & Restaurant (East Aurora): 652-4221

Millard Fillmore House (East Aurora): 652-0167

Roycroft Campus Antiques (East Aurora): 655-1565

Roycroft Potters (East Aurora): 652-7422

Elbert Hubbard Museum (East Aurora): 652-3280

Vidler's 5 & 10 (East Aurora): 652-0481

Toy Town Museum (East Aurora): 655-3891

Baker Memorial Church (East Aurora): 652-0500

Old Orchard Inn (East Aurora): 652-4664

The Tea Cozy (Wales Center): 655-3304

Letchworth State Park (Castile): 493-2611 or 800-456-2267

Glen Iris Inn (Letchworth State Park): 493-2622

National Warplane Museum (Geneseo): 243-0690

Genesee Country Museum (Mumford): 538-6822

Genesee Country Inn (Mumford): 538-4565

12 ~

Niagara

From points east and south: Take the New York Thruway to Niagara Falls to the Robert Moses Parkway to Lewiston. From points north, take the Robert Moses Parkway to Lewiston.

Highlights: *Niagara Falls, historic village, performing arts, Lake Ontario, orchards, salmon fishing, cobblestone buildings, scenery, and pick-your-own farms.*

This is a day trip ideal for visitors who have come to see Niagara Falls and want to see what's beyond the mighty waterfall. Almost nothing can match the falls for its awesome power and spectacle. Don't miss a visit even if you have visited before—Niagara remains an incredible natural wonder. Beyond the falls there's the historic village of Lewiston and Artpark, the only state park for the performing arts, Youngstown at the mouth of Niagara River, Fort Niagara, Lake Ontario, orchards, world-class salmon fishing, the highest concentration of cobblestone buildings in the world, dramatic vistas, and pick-your-own farms. This tour makes a circle beginning and ending in Lewiston.

Niagara Falls actually had its origins 12,000 years ago, seven miles north of its present location, in what is now the village of Lewiston. The falls continue to creep upstream at a rate of an inch or so a year. In 1974 Artpark was opened in the village on 200 acres overlooking the river. It's the only state park in the United States devoted to the visual and performing arts.

The critically acclaimed Buffalo Philharmonic Orchestra plays here, along with other musical and theatrical performers, during the ten-week summer season. The back wall of the Artpark Theater opens for evening performances, allowing lawn seating and spectacular views of the Niagara River gorge, especially at sunset. Picnicking on the lawn before concerts is popular. During the rest of the year, Artpark stages a variety of events at Artpark-at-the-Church, formerly St. Peter's Roman Catholic Church, just two blocks from the Artpark entrance.

Sculptors and others artists are in residence. You can sit at the feet of a storyteller in the woods, don a mask and join a company of actors, watch your child create a puppet, or try your hand at oriental brush painting. You'll also find a fishing dock and hiking trails. Guided tours of the park's geological sites are provided by the Schoellkopf Museum.

A most historic site, this is where Seneca Indians, French, British, and Americans fought for control of the strategically important Niagara River. Here also are relics of Hopewell Indians, who lived on the site 4,000 years ago. An Indian burial mound is listed in the National Register of Historic Places. Across the river is Canada and the village of Queenston.

From the upper levels of Artpark and the Niagara escarpment, you can look down to the lower Niagara River and the Lewiston landing. This spot was the ideal place to land boats and cargo to be carried overland around the turbulent rapids and cataracts of Niagara Falls—the main barrier in the natural water route from the Atlantic to the Mississippi.

Centuries before the white man arrived, Indians landed their canoes here to begin the famed portage. The first Europeans to discover Niagara Falls, explorers LaSalle and Father Hennepin, landed here in 1678.

Control of the lower Niagara signified control of the Great Lakes. For the next century, the area was fought over by the Iroquois, French, and British. With the Revolution came American control, and Lewiston thrived. A tramway, built here by the British to carry goods up to the escarpment, was America's first railroad.

It was during this time, according to local legend, that Catherine Hustler, proprietress of a tavern on Center Street, poured some gin and herbed wine into a tankard, plucked the tail feather of a stuffed cock pheasant to stir it with, and served the first cocktail.

For many years the Frontier House, built in 1824, welcomed weary travelers. Now it's America's only McDonald's in a registered National Landmark. Lewiston lies in the midst of fruit orchards, and during the first weekend in September there's a Peach Festival with parades, peach blossoms, peach fuzz, and queen contests. You will find games, rides, and peach shortcake galore.

Leaving Lewiston, take State 104 east through farm country. Just outside the village the road skirts the Tuscarora Indian Reservation. Continue through the countryside to the hamlet of Wrights Corners. Turn south on State 78 into Lockport, the second largest city in the county but very much a small town. It was named for the canal locks in the town. The Marquis de Lafayette, French hero of the American Revolution, visited in 1825 and proclaimed that "Lockport and the County of Niagara contain the greatest natural and artificial wonders."

If you want to see the canal locks up close, the best way to do it is by taking an excursion with Lockport Locks and Canal Tours, which operates from May to November. The 363-mile Erie Canal connects the Hudson River with the Niagara River. Originally dug by hand, eighty-three stone locks were used to overcome the 571-foot difference in the levels of the two rivers. The canal was renovated in 1915, and thirty-five locks now allow larger vessels to travel between the Atlantic Ocean and the Great Lakes. Tours let cruisers experience "locking through" Locks 34 and 35 and being raised 49.5 feet to overcome the difference in elevation of the Niagara escarpment. The canal boat travels under lift bridges that raise straight up and the "Upside-down" railroad bridge.

Back on State 104, continue east. This road features more cobblestone buildings than any other road in the world, according to Bill Lattin, director of the Cobblestone Museum in Childs. This is a unique form of regional architecture that owes its existence to the Erie Canal. Many masons were recruited from England to lay up stonework for the locks. When their job was done, in 1828, they were out of work. They sold a local resident on the idea of having a house with walls of cobble, much like those back in southeastern England, where many of the Erie Canal masons hailed from.

The walls of the homes are faced with thousands of small, water-rounded stones picked from the beaches of nearby Lake Ontario or from fields and gravel pits. The stones are laid in rows, creating buildings with fascinating textured walls of rock and masonry. Once the first homes went up, the idea caught on and dozens more were put up around the countryside.

It's fun to watch the evolution of the cobbles. Early ones are easily spotted because the walls have fairly large, uneven-sized, variously colored stones. Styles evolved and stones of more uniform color and size were used. In the last stages of cobblestone house making, just before the Civil War, stones were very uniform and small, about the size of a hen's egg, and have the same reddish color. These homes were the most labor-intensive of all. Some masons used alternate rows of red and white stone to make stripes. Others put patterns of black stones among the reddish brown ones. If cobbles were in short supply, the back wall of the house was often made up of regular fieldstone.

At the intersection of State 104 and State 98 in Childs is the Cobblestone Museum—actually several cobblestone buildings, which form the nucleus of the museum. The museum's centerpiece is its handsome Universalist Church, built in 1834, which once served time as a cabbage storehouse. History-minded volunteers saved the building from such ignominy. Other buildings were added to the roster of "stone piles," including the Ward House beside the church and Gaines District No. 5 schoolhouse just down the road. The museum is open Tuesdays through Sundays during the summer.

From Childs it's just a short drive (about three miles) north on State 98 to Lake Ontario and the Seaway Trail. Here you will find beaches, marinas, and two state parks with facilities for camping, picnicking, fishing, and boating. Although there are health department advisories regarding eating the fish caught in Lake Ontario because of contamination from lake and river chemical plants, sport fishermen flock here for record-breaking salmon.

Take the Seaway Trail (State 18 here) west. The road passes through lush orchards and past roadside stands brimming with the bounty of the land. The farther west the road goes, the closer it hugs the lake. Stop at the Somerset Lighthouse at Golden Hill State Park. There are several shipwrecks here from the 1600s. The lighthouse is built of hand-carved stone. A circular staircase allows visitors to climb to the top for a panoramic view. Wilson is a popular fishing mecca and boasts several beaches.

Continue on to Fort Niagara State Park and Old Fort Niagara. Located at the mouth of Niagara River and overlooking Lake Ontario, the fort has a commanding view of the river

*Lake Ontario's
Somerset Lighthouse
built of hand-carved
stone*

and Lake Ontario. On a clear day, visitors can see across the lake to downtown Toronto in Canada with the city's signature CN Tower and the SkyDome. They appear to be a kind of mirage from a future world.

The fort controlled access to the Great Lakes during colonial times. Its strategic value diminished with the completion of the Erie Canal, yet it remained an active military fort into the early twentieth century. The fort's original stone buildings have been preserved as they were before the American Revolution. French Castle, the oldest building in the Great Lakes area, was built in 1726. Military reenactments, battles, grand reviews, tent camps, fifes and drums, crafts, and archaeological digs are scheduled throughout the year. The flags of the French, British, and Americans have flown over this fort. Each of these nations sought the support of a powerful fourth nation, the Iroquois Confederacy.

There are guided tours of the fort. In the guard tower, a costumed interpreter explains that about fourteen men lived here, sharing common bunks, and that each spent every third day on guard duty. That meant remaining in uniform for twenty-four hours, spending two hours on guard, and four hours off, around the clock. Special events happen throughout the year, including the King's Birthday, French and Indian War, Eighteenth-Century Family Days, Soldiers of the Revolution, War of 1812 Days, Civil War Artillery School, and more. A resident ghost reportedly haunts the fort.

The village of Youngstown has a nautical flavor with a bustling yacht club and waterside eateries. Continue south along State 18F, which follows the Niagara River and is still part of the Seaway Trail. Joseph Davis State Park is a pleasant spot for an afternoon visit, especially on a warm summer day. The big attractions are a double Olympic-size swimming pool, a separate diving pool, and a wading pool. Playground equipment is bountiful and there's a park nature trail. The park is open in the winter for cross-country skiing.

Then it's back to Lewiston and the circle is complete.

In the Area

All numbers are in area code 716.

Artpark (Lewiston): 754-9000 or 800-659-PARK

Artpark-at-the-Church (Lewiston): 754-4375

Schoellkopf Geological Museum (Niagara Falls): 278-1780

Lockport Locks and Canal Tours (Lockport): 693-3260

Cobblestone Museum (Childs): 589-9510

Somerset Lighthouse (Somerset): 795-3885

Fort Niagara State Park (Youngstown): 745-7273

Old Fort Niagara (Youngstown): 745-7611

Joseph Davis State Park (Lewiston): 754-4596

13 ~

Farm Country: US 62

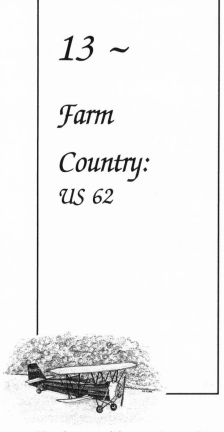

South of Buffalo: Take the New York Thruway to the Hamburg exit to the village of Hamburg and US 62 (South Park Avenue).

Highlights: *One of the country's largest county fairs, lush farm fields, roadside stands, kazoo factory, pumpkins, Amish country.*

Hamburg, a fifteen-minute drive south of the city of Buffalo, has an old-fashioned air. Century-old houses line the streets. It bills itself as "the town that friendship built."

Every August since 1821, thousands flock to the Erie County Fair on US 62 in Hamburg. It was here, in 1885, that the hamburger was born. Frank Menches, a concessionaire at the fair, was ready to cook his specialty, a pork sausage sandwich. The local meat market had run out of pork sausage, so he returned with five pounds of chopped meat. Menches formed the beef into patties and cooked it up on his stove. The result was tasty and tempting. Thus was born and christened

117

the hamburger, which was to become America's favorite sandwich.

The fair, which bills itself as "America's County Fair," is one of the largest county fairs in the nation. It regularly attracts more than 800,000 fairgoers during its eleven-day run. It features everything that makes a county fair such a meaningful piece of Americana: tractor pulls, demolition derbies, cow, goat, sheep, and horse shows, 4-H auctions, competitions for the best fruits and vegetables, parades, food, food, and more food, and top-name entertainment.

Just outside the village is the tiny hamlet of Water Valley and the Water Valley Inn, a good place to sample a Buffalo-area speciality—beef-on-weck sandwiches—thinly sliced roast beef piled high on fresh kimmelweck rolls.

US 62 next passes through Eden, which calls itself the "Garden Spot of New York State." The rich soils are remarkably fertile and generations of farm families have been growing prize-winning tomatoes, potatoes, and other vegetables in this lush valley.

Stop at Braymiller's Market for a taste of the fresh fruits and vegetables grown in the area. The ice-cream cones made with Charlaps Ice Cream, from a local dairy, are delicious and huge—a single scoop is like a double or triple one anywhere else.

If you are interested in original art works of the area, especially scenes of the Amish community, take a detour just after Braymiller's and turn left on State 75. Turn left on Hardt Road and go to the end to East Eden Road. Turn right and look for the sign that says "Thelma Winter, Artist." This retired music teacher creates lovely paintings using pen-and-ink and watercolors.

Time out for a stop at a real American original—The Original American Kazoo Company. It was established in 1916 and is now the only metal kazoo factory in the world.

This renovated building bills itself as the kazoo capital of the world.

The miniature museum highlights history and amusing trivia and shows how kazoos are made. Kazoos of all shapes and sizes are on display. The collection chronicles their history and includes a wooden kazoo similar to the one that served as a model for the metal prototype; liquor bottle-shaped kazoos that celebrated the end of Prohibition; antique and instrument kazoos.

The factory, which is visible from behind a half-rail in the museum, continues to manufacture a complete line of kazoos. They are made the same way today as in 1916. The machines that make kazoos are the same die presses that were installed in 1907, when the building housed a sheet-metal workshop. They were used to produce everything from toy flutes and fishing tackle-boxes to metal dog beds and peanut vending machines. In 1965, demand for kazoos became so great that the manufacturing of the other items ceased. The Smithsonian lists the kazoo as the only original American musical instrument. You are invited to sign a petition to make the kazoo America's national musical instrument.

The gift shop is filled with unusual items, including children's books and toys and, of course, a variety of kazoos to complete or start your very own kazoo band. A record was set in nearby Rochester on January 2, 1986, when 54,500 kazooists set a record for the greatest number of people to play kazoos.

The next stop is Collins. At first glance it may appear to be a typical small farming town like many others that dot the state. But don't be fooled. This is the home of Ray Waterman and his gigantic pumpkins and the hometown of the World Pumpkin Confederation.

We are talking about pumpkins in excess of 800 pounds here. Waterman himself won the top prize for a 780.5-pound pumpkin in 1991. However, thus far the world record is a 827-pound pumpkin from the state of Washington. The dream of Waterman and his pumpkin-growing compatriots is a 1,000-pound pumpkin by the turn of the century.

The very best time to pass through town is the first Saturday in October, when the World Pumpkin Weigh-Off is held at Waterman's Restaurant. You will know you have picked the right day because of the crowds. This is a genuine happening and because of Waterman's marketing flair, newspapers and magazines around the world have taken note of Collins and the pumpkin weigh-off.

If you are serious about growing big pumpkins, you can subscribe to the confederation newsletter and read Waterman's messages, which he signs *Peace through Pumpkins*. It might seem like an inflated view of pumpkins, but an argument could be made that if the whole world was engaged in

Finalists can tip the scales at 800 pounds or more

growing giant pumpkins then there would not be any time for wars—or much else.

Even if you are not into growing giant pumpkins, or giant squash, or giant beets, or giant sunflowers, or giant kohlrabi (there are prizes for giants in all these categories), the contest is something to see.

Huge forklifts gently lift the behemoths onto scales. Children pose for photographs sitting on the pumpkins or standing beside them. Someone always brings a tiny baby and poses with the baby sleeping peacefully on the biggest pumpkin.

There are pumpkin T-shirts, jackets, bumper stickers, seeds from certified giants, smaller, more reasonably sized pumpkins for sale to be made into jack-o-lanterns or pies. Bands play and American flags wave in the breeze. Upstairs in Waterman's, a conference call gathers information about the giants from New Zealand, South Africa, Canada, California, and other parts of the globe that are vying for top pumpkin honors.

If you miss the weigh-off, Waterman's Restaurant is still a good place to stop for good home-style cooking at reasonable prices. You can buy the pumpkin seeds in the gift shop.

US 62 in the Collins area runs parallel to the borders of the Cattaraugus Indian Reservation. It's a popular stop for bingo players because of the large payoffs and for gas and cigarette purchases because of the absence of taxes, although New York state is fighting the reservation on this issue.

The next village is Gowanda, half in Erie County and half in Cattaraugus County. The village is divided by Cattaraugus Creek and was first settled in 1810 by Turner Aldrich, according to the historical marker alongside the creek.

If you want to take a break from driving and still view the countryside, there are rail excursions originating from the

New York & Lake Erie Railroad station on Commercial Street. The excursions operate year-round, although autumn provides the most glorious views of the countryside awash in color.

As you continue your drive south on US 62, road markers with buggies on them begin to appear. These signs serve two purposes. They are a quiet announcement that you are in Amish country, and they warn drivers to look out for horse-drawn buggies.

This is Amish country. The Amish make up a significant portion of the population of the Conewango Valley. They form a society within a society—forsaking all the so-called advances of the twentieth century. It's easy to tell which homes belong to the Amish. You'll see a buggy or two in the driveway and no electric lines connecting to the house. The Amish do not use cars or tractors on their farms, or electricity of any kind. They do not have radios or television sets. They are living much as their eighteenth-century forebears did.

The Amish are farmers and woodworkers. The women make rugs and quilts, by hand, of course, just as their foremothers have for the past 200 years. The Amish farmers sell their milk to Mueller's Valley View Cheese Factory in Conewango Valley. Stop in for a sample of some of the forty varieties.

The Amish of the Conewango Valley are largely undiscovered and have not become a tourist attraction. Men are always dressed in black and women wear long skirts and bonnets. They limit their interactions with the "other world," although they are happy to sell their handmade wares. Occasionally, if a family incurs large medical expenses, they will sponsor a craft fair with a large assortment of quilts, baked goods, and furniture for sale. Otherwise, they do not sell anything on Sundays, and they do not approve of visitors (or anyone else) taking their photos.

Just beyond the cheese factory, look for a hand-lettered sign that says "Wooden Rockers." Turn right on Young Road and continue up into the hills until you spot another sign and then turn right on Flatiron. At the first house, stop if you are interested in handmade bentwood hickory rockers or footstools. Usually, you will have to place an order. No deposit required, of course. The price is much less than that of similar rockers sold in mail-order catalogs. There is something special about meeting and dealing directly with the craftsperson who makes your furniture. The chairs are very comfortable and well made.

Drive back down to US 62 and continue into the village of Conewango Valley. Stop at the Amish Country Fair, a gift shop with a good selection of locally made toys, quilts, crafts, and furniture. If you spot something you like, you can buy it on the spot.

Next door, stop in the photo store, where you can pick up a copy of *Dogshire Times*, a newsletter of the valley. An ad in the newsletter promoted the Reynolds Restaurant on Main Street, which promises, "We give you more for less." The daily specials for $2.57 plus tax are a real bargain, and good, too. Specials include chicken and biscuits with applesauce. This is an early town, for Reynolds opens at 6:00 A.M. and closes at 8:00 P.M.

These are ideal country roads for real country-road devotees. Take your pick and drive down any narrow two-lane road running off US 62. East and West Road, just beyond the intersection of US 62 and State 241, was a good choice.

Most of the farms along the road are Amish. Around the first turn we saw an Amish farmer working the fields with his horses. The paved road turned to an unpaved but still smooth road. The sound of hoofs was getting closer. A horse-drawn buggy was quickly driven down the road. Another one passed by, going in the opposite direction.

Signs tacked to poles offer quilts, rugs, and furniture. You'll see a one-room schoolhouse for the Amish children of the valley who generally go to school until the eighth grade and have a special exemption from the mandatory school-attendance rules.

Back on US 62, the road continues to the village of Ellington. Clear Creek Carriages has antique carriages and offers sleigh rides along with organic plants and produce for sale.

US 62 continues down to the New York-Pennsylvania border and into Pennsylvania.

In the Area

All numbers are in area code 716.

Erie County Fair (Hamburg): 649-3900

Water Valley Inn (Water Valley): 649-9691

Braymiller's Market (Hamburg): 649-2356

Thelma Winter (Eden): 992-4277

American Kazoo Company (Eden): 992-3960

Waterman's Restaurant (Collins): 532-5995

New York & Lake Erie Railroad (Gowanda): 532-5242

Mueller's Valley View Cheese Factory (Conewango Valley): 296-5711

Amish Country Fair (Conewango Valley): 287-3975

Reynolds Restaurant (Conewango Valley): 287-3899

Clear Creek Carriages (Ellington): 287-2719

World Pumpkin Confederation Newsletter (Collins): 532-3260

14 ~

Chautauqua

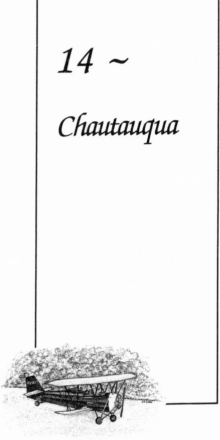

Take the New York Thruway south of Buffalo, about forty-two miles to thruway exit 59 and Dunkirk.

Highlights: *Wineries, lakes, inns, antiques, world spiritualism center.*

Although many come to the Chautauqua Institution, the area's oldest and most famous summer gathering place, for the entire summer, it is possible to meander along country roads and visit most attractions in a weekend. You'll find wineries, lakes—three in all—country inns, antique shops, and the world center of spiritualism. This tour makes a complete circle through Chautauqua County, the state's westernmost county, beginning and ending in Dunkirk.

Dunkirk, so named because the harbor resembled that of Dunkerque, France, is the starting point for this tour, which will especially appeal to water lovers. The highpoint in Dunkirk history probably was in 1851, when the New York & Lake Erie Railroad completed the laying of its lines from New York to Dunkirk, an accomplishment that was celebrated with great festivity. It was the longest railroad in the world at the time.

Stop at the Dunkirk Lighthouse, which was built in 1826 to help protect shipping on Lake Erie. The keeper is gone now and the light is automated, but it still serves an important function. The whole facility is also a museum, listed in the Register of Historic Places. It celebrates both the history and importance of the light and honors the armed forces of the United States.

The Veterans Museum occupies six rooms of the keeper's house, with one room devoted to each of the five services. Another room honors the lighthouse keepers and displays memorabilia from days gone by. A cast-iron spiral stairway leads to a ten-sided lantern, measuring eight feet three inches across each face.

Just inland from Dunkirk is Fredonia (take State 83). It was settled in 1803 and in 1821 America's first gas well was sunk here. A large boulder marks the site. In 1825 when the Marquis de Lafayette and his son, George Washington Lafayette, visited, the streets were lighted with gas lamps. In 1873 the Women's Christian Temperance Union was formed here, an area that ironically now is the center for wine production.

The White Inn, at 52 East Main Street, is the oldest continually operating hotel in the county. The inn is named in honor of Squire White, one of the earliest settlers of the county and its first physician. It occupies his homesite, encompassing the Victorian home built by his son Devillo in 1868 on the site of the original frame structure.

Since it was taken over by a pair of philosophy professors at Fredonia State College who are well versed in the art of renovation and restoration, the inn has been trans-formed back to its glory days. Rooms are filled with antiques and period reproductions made in nearby Jamestown. In 1935 the inn was designated a charter member of the elite Duncan Hines Family of Fine Restaurants. Award-winning chefs serve old favorites and imaginative dishes, including a flourless chocolate cake that attracts chocoholics from near and far.

More than a century ago, Fredonia was known as the world's seed capital, and the Fredonia Seed Company is still operating. This is also the home of Red Wing Foods, producer of peanut butter that has achieved a certain celebrity status. It is a favorite of actor Charlton Heston and writer William F. Buckley, who journeyed here to christen the company's new peanut roaster.

If your timing is right (generally June and early July for strawberries and July through September for raspberries), head north on US 20 outside Fredonia to State 39 for one mile to the Berry Bush, where you can pick your own strawberries and raspberries or buy fresh-picked berries. Actually, just about every road on this route will yield up roadside stands brimming over with the harvest of area farmers.

Heading back, take Center Road west to King Road and the Merritt Estate Winery, where tours and tastings of award-winning wines are offered daily.

Continue back on Center Road to US 20 through Fredonia to Westfield. This route passes through Brocton, the site of the area's first grape culture back in 1824.

Just before Westfield, stop at Vetter Vineyards on East Main Road (US 20) for wine tastings. Tours are offered during the summer. Westfield is the self-proclaimed "Grape Juice Capital of the World" and the home of Welch's Foods. It was founded by Charles Edgar Welch, who declared that "God did not mean the grape to be fermented." The visitors center in the center of town offers free grape juice. Westfield is also a mecca for antique lovers.

The favorite story of Westfield residents is that of the little girl who persuaded Abraham Lincoln to grow a beard. During the presidential campaign of 1860, eleven-year-old Grace Bedell wrote to the smooth-shaven Lincoln that she thought he would be much better looking with whiskers. Lincoln wrote back to her and told her he was going to take her advice. On February 15, 1861, when Lincoln's train stopped in the village on his way to Washington and his inauguration, he greeted the crowd and told them the story of Grace and his new beard. He called for her to come forward and then jumped from the platform, kissed her, pointed to his whiskers and said, "You see, I have followed your advice."

High on a grassy knoll overlooking Lake Erie (on State 394—2.6 miles from US 20) is the William Seward Inn, built in 1821. It was the home of William Henry Seward, then a young attorney from Auburn, who later served as Lincoln's secretary of state and was responsible for the purchase of Alaska. Seward was in Westfield as an agent for the Holland Land Company, which bought thousands of acres in the area from Robert Morris, "the financier of the American Revolution." The home used to stand in town, near the railroad station, but in 1966 it was moved to this more majestic site.

Westfield is just inland from the historic Barcelona Harbor. Its 1828 lighthouse was the first in the world to be lighted by natural gas.

If you wish to take a short detour for wine tastings continue south on US 20 just a few miles to the Johnson Estate Winery, one of the excellent small wineries in the area. Tastings are offered daily and tours are available in the summer. The Schloss Doepken Winery on Old US 20 is just a couple of miles farther south. Tastings and sales are available from June 1 to November 1.

Back in Westfield, take State 394 five miles southeast to Lake Chautauqua. The county takes its name from its largest lake, which is twenty-two miles long. Chautauqua Lake was called Jad-dah-gwah by the Indians. French explorers landed on the county's Lake Erie shoreline in 1679. Their quest was a southward passage to the Ohio and Mississippi rivers. The route connecting Barcelona Harbor on Lake Erie with Chautauqua Lake, later known as the Portage Trail, offered an answer. The controversy between France and England over possession of the trail led to the French and Indian War, and played a part in Europe's Seven Years' War.

Just five miles along State 394 from the head of the lake is the area's oldest and greatest cultural asset—the Chautauqua Institution. It was here, on the shores of the lake in 1874, that John Heyl Vincent, a Methodist minister, and industrialist Lewis Miller began a training center for Sunday school teachers. Their dream was a two-week meeting at which teachers could vacation in canvas tents, listen to self-improvement lectures by the light of pine-knot torches, and stroll by the lakeshore.

But the founders had a bigger vision for Chautauqua, according to the institution's historian and former editor of the *Daily Chautauquan*, Alfreda L. Irwin. She has been coming to Chautauqua for more than seventy years and wrote the history of this unique place.

> Their vision centered around education, and for a period in the late nineteenth century the institution was chartered as a university. Students came here in the summer, and during the rest of the year they took courses by correspondence. . . . What is so special about Chautauqua is the blend of the arts, music, education, religion and sports. We had one of the first physical education schools in the country and we pioneered the idea of correspondence schools.

The celebrated Chautauqua Literary and Scientific Circle, the oldest continuous book club in America, began as a home reading program to enable those deprived of formal education to acquire "the college outlook." The circle was the forerunner of correspondence courses and book clubs and inspired Chautauqua societies throughout the United States. It also played a major role in the establishment of adult education. *Chautauqua* became a household word across the country as tent-show proprietors crisscrossed the hinterlands with their own version of Chautauqua's lectures, music, and drama. Today, the Chautauqua circuit is part of history, but the institution is very much alive.

President Theodore Roosevelt, who visited five times, called the institution "the most American place in America."

The Chautauqua Institution is a National Register Historic District and occupies 856 acres. Many of the early Victorian buildings are still standing in all their gingerbread glory. The new condos that are springing up on the grounds and nearby are designed to blend into the nineteenth-century ambience. The grand dame of all the Chautauqua buildings is the Athenaeum Hotel, built in 1881 and wired for electricity by Lewis Miller's son-in-law—Thomas Alva Edison.

"This is where he sat," said W. Thomas Smith, hotel manager. The table was next to a large window that extends to the floor, permitting easy access to the veranda that nearly encircles the hotel. "Edison was a shy man, who would come in through the open window and leave the same way. He wanted to avoid the admirers waiting outside the dining room door."

Edison, whose friends at Chautauqua included Henry Ford and Harvey Firestone, was one of many famous people to speak or vacation at the facility. Nine U.S. presidents have done so—starting with Ulysses S. Grant—as have Leo Tolstoy, William Jennings Bryan, John Philip Sousa, and a who's-who in the fields of literature, music, dance, and theater, as well as science, politics, business, and religion.

The Athenaeum Hotel at Chautauqua

Psychologist William James called the institution "the middle-class paradise, without a sin, without a victim, without a blot, without a tear." From the beginning, alcohol of any sort was banned, and it is still not sold on the grounds, although guests may partake in their rooms. Over the years, whenever the subject of alcohol was brought up, the board decided that it was best not to tamper with what many considered a fundamental part of the institution.

Although there have been some changes over the years, to visit Chautauqua is to enter an older, more placid, America. The streets are short, and many are paved with bricks. They are lined with old wooden homes, many of which have three tiers of balconies and an American flag out front. The tranquil atmosphere is helped by barring vehicles from the fenced-in grounds. You can obtain a pass for your car only at the beginning and end of your stay to unload and pick up luggage. For the rest of the time, vehicles remain in lots outside the gates.

Near one of the three swimming beaches is Palestine Park, a 350-foot-long model of the Holy Land intended to teach biblical geography. Chautauqua Lake represents the Mediterranean, reversing the points of the compass. The model is built to scale with a twenty-foot-long Dead Sea and a rock-sculpted Bethlehem.

Tradition is something that perennial visitors can count on. Many visitors are repeaters, and second-, third-, fourth-, and even sixth- or seventh-generation visitors are not uncommon. The institution strives to appeal to all ages by offering a mix of arts, education, religion, and recreation during the nine-week summer season. There are day camps for children. Classrooms enroll more than 2,000 people of all ages in subjects from archaeology to Zen. Popular, nationally known entertainers pack the 6,000-seat amphitheater, which also overflows for Sunday religious services.

Only at Chautauqua can a visitor fish for record-breaking muskellunge in the morning, attend a midmorning lecture by a major speaker on world peace, play a round of golf in the afternoon, study music before dinner, and after dinner enjoy a concert in the open-air amphitheater or an opera in Norton Memorial Hall. The sounds of rehearsal are everywhere, from the cluster of sheds where violinists and pianists practice to the acoustically magnificent amphitheater, recital halls, and the Athenaeum lounge. George Gershwin wrote his *Concerto in F* in one of the practice sheds.

Although the institution is officially open only during the nine-week summer season, some of the hotels and condos are available during the rest of the year. Fall and winter can be particularly lovely along the shores of Lake Chautauqua. Horse-drawn sleigh rides are available during weekends in the winter.

In keeping with the nineteenth-century atmosphere, a paddle wheeler, *Chautauqua Belle*, offers cruises around the lake. Since 1811, the Stow-Bemus Point Ferry has been ferrying passengers and vehicles across the narrowest part of the lake. Back in its early days, the paddle wheel on the ferry was powered by an ox on a treadmill. Today, the diesel-powered ferry carries nine cars and fifty passengers. Much to the dismay of some preservationists, a bridge was built across the lake, but the ferry is still in service during the summer and offers a six-minute ride across the narrows.

Continue on State 394 south from the institution to Stow for the ferry to Bemus Point, an old-fashioned lakeside community. Before taking the ferry across the lake, stop at the Good Morning Farm. The farm is a restaurant featuring home cooking using produce gathered from neighboring farms and a country store housed in a 150-year-old barn. Right at the Bemus Point Ferry Landing is the Casino with a museum, beach, park, boat launch, and dock. The Casino ballroom welcomes dancers with the sounds of Big Bands on selected nights during the summer.

Comedienne Lucille Ball was born and grew up in Jamestown at the end of the lake. She began her career on the stages of the Shea's and Palace theaters in Jamestown. The annual Lucille Ball Festival of New Comedy, held late in May, has been created in her honor. Her daughter, Luci, has helped kick off the festival.

If your timing is right and you are a rodeo enthusiast, take State 60 north of Jamestown for six miles to the village of Gerry, home of the "oldest Consecutive Rodeo East of the Mississippi." Presented by the Gerry Volunteer Fire Department, it's held during the first week in August and features professional riders, midway rides, and the much acclaimed Western Beef Barbecue.

Otherwise, back in Bemus Point, take State 44 to Ellery Center and State 57 north to Centralia. From there, take State 380 north to Stockton. Once in the village of Stockton, turn left at the blinking light onto Mill Street. Millrace Park is on the right and just beyond is Stockton Sales, a wondrous establishment made up of five barns overflowing with antiques, collectibles, and stuff—handmade baskets, barber poles, a mounted water-buffalo head, carousel horses, pianos, sofas, clocks, books, china, oriental rugs—all from estates throughout New York, Ohio, and Pennsylvania. True collectors have been known to spend the better part of a day in the Stockton Sales barns.

After this shopping detour, take State 58 two miles north to Cassadaga. In this largely rural corner of the state, eccentricity seems to thrive. Just five years after the founding of the Chautauqua Institution, the Lily Dale Assembly was started in 1879 on the shores of Cassadaga Lake. Lily Dale is the spiritualist center of the world and every summer it attracts mediums from all over the United States and Canada. They claim to put visitors in touch with the "other side." There are certain similarities with the better-known and more mainstream Chautauqua Institution, including the bookstore, library, lecture halls, and cottage-lined streets radiating from a lovely lake.

That's where the similarities end, however. The signs in front of the Lily Dale cottages advertise "mediums" who are willing to give a reading. According to a workshop schedule, at least thirty mediums are "tested, approved and registered by the Lily Dale Assembly." Lily Dale is open during the late-June-to-early-September summer season and workshops concentrate on spiritual self-help. A cathedral of sorts with church pews is sheltered by towering oaks. A message service is available for those who believe in communicating with the dead.

From Lily Dale continue north on State 60 about nine miles back to Dunkirk to complete your circle.

In the Area

All numbers are in area code 716.

Dunkirk Historical Lighthouse (Dunkirk): 366-5050

The White Inn (Fredonia): 672-2103

The Berry Bush (Forestville): 679-1240

Merritt Estate Winery (Forestville): 965-4800

Vetter Vineyards (Westfield): 326-3100

William Seward Inn (Westfield): 326-4151 or 800-338-4151

Johnson Estate Winery (Westfield): 326-2191

Schloss Doepken Winery (Ripley): 326-3636

Chautauqua Institution (Chautauqua): 357-6200 or
    800-836-ARTS

Chautauqua Belle Cruises (Mayville): 753-2403

Good Morning Farm (Stow): 763-1773
The Casino (Bemus Point): 386-3661
Lucille Ball Festival of New Comedy (Jamestown): 484-7070
Gerry Rodeo (Gerry): 985-4847
Stockton Sales (Stockton): 595-3516
Lily Dale Assembly (Lily Dale): 595-8721

Index

Other titles in the Country Roads Series:

Country Roads of Connecticut and Rhode Island
Country Roads of Florida
Country Roads of Hawaii
Country Roads of Illinois, second edition
Country Roads of Indiana
Country Roads of Kentucky
Country Roads of the Maritimes
Country Roads of Massachusetts
Country Roads of Michigan, second edition
Country Roads of New Jersey
Country Roads of New Hampshire
Country Roads of New York
Country Days In New York City
Country Roads of North Carolina
Country Roads of Ohio
Country Roads of Ontario
Country Roads of Oregon
Country Roads of Pennsylvania
Country Roads of Quebec
Country Roads of Tennessee
Country Roads of Vermont
Country Roads of Virginia
Country Roads of Washington

All books are $9.95 at bookstores.
Or order directly from the publisher (add $3.00
shipping & handling for direct orders):
Country Roads Press
P.O. Box 286
Castine, Maine 04421
Toll-free phone number: **800-729-9179**